I0752971

Cuba Today

Cuba Today

images of a nation on the cusp of change

photography by

michael nelson

introduction by **louis e.v. nevaer**

This book will be updated annually, and subsequent editions will reflect corrections, updates and changes in the opinions, conclusions and recommendations for firms offering goods and services to the public. The book is also available as an electronic book at Amazon.com.

Publication date: July 2016.

These photographs are available for sale from the photographer. For more information, please contact Michael Nelson at:

Michael Nelson
Website: www.michaeldalenelson.com
Email: michael@michaeldalenelson.com
Telephone: (845) 534-4563

Published by Ediciones del Mayab
Calle 59 # 572 x 72
Colonia Centro
Mérida, Yucatán
MEXICO
Facebook: https://www.facebook.com/ediciones.delmayab

ISBN: 978-1-939879-23-3

Cover and Interior Design by John Clifton
john@johnclifton.net

Contents

Cuba, on the Cusp of Change

Hearts are broken every day.

When U.S. President Barack Obama traveled to Havana on March 21, 2016, the first visit by a sitting American president to the Caribbean island nation in 88 years, he arrived to an island of broken hearts.

That's the melancholy of the Cuban reality.

Broken promises. Broken dreams. Broken hearts.

The despair is seen in the unloved buildings that reflect decades of social and political upheaval, where multitudes of Cubans were forced to abandon their homeland against their will. It is seen in the faces of Cuba's youth, anxious for the past to be put far behind them and for their "future" to begin. It is also seen in the long lines of Cubans at embassies throughout Havana who, not willing to let life pass them by, are desperate for a visa that will let them leave.

The broken hearted leaving Cuba has become part of government euphemisms throughout the island: "When so-and-so abandoned the country, this building became public property."

If Cuba reflects the sadness of a grand sociopolitical experiment that has withered under the tropical sun, there is quiet resignation with dark undertones. "I'll make you a Cuba libre," the bartender at the Capri Hotel says. "Because it's the most ironic drink I can make you."

Hearts *are* broken every day.

The first heart Fidel Castro broke, ironically, was not a Cuban's.

On July 7, 1955 Fidel Castro abandoned Havana, exiled to Mexico by Fulgencio Batista. He boarded Mexicana de Aviación Flight 566 and landed in Mérida, the largest city in the Yucatán peninsula.

He arrived in Mexico as a tourist using the name "Alejandro González." He would leave as Fidel Castro, insurgent.

From Mérida, he continued to Mexico City to rendezvous with other revolutionaries. During the eighteen months he spent in exile in Mexico, however, he would return to Mérida, at first on reconnaissance missions, and then because he met a young woman with whom he fell in love: Lía Cámara Blum.

She was eighteen years old, a young teacher. She spotted him at the bus station in Valladolid. Fidel Castro was traveling throughout the peninsula, careful to evade Batista's spies who were everywhere. He had traveled to Cozumel, near Isla Holbox, and throughout the mainland of the peninsula. He wanted to determine if the

Yucatán was suitable for launching an attack on Cuba. Having concluded that leaving from either Cozumel or the ports of the Mexican Caribbean would be too risky, he was taking the bus to Mérida.

When he boarded that bus on a Saturday afternoon in Valladolid, Lía Cámara Blum, a passenger, stared at Fidel Casto as he walked down the aisle. She was a teacher in the provincial town of Tizimín and was going home to visit her family for the weekend.

"He's not from here," she told herself, drawn to the Cuban exile the moment they first made eye contact.

She smiled at him. He smiled back.

Then he sat next to her, introduced himself as "Alejandro González," and, after finding out she was a teacher, asked if she minded talking about history. "Of course," she said. Then he began to ask her about the Mexican Revolution.

They immediately liked each other.

He found her intelligent and well-spoken. She found him polite, well-educated, and inquisitive. She told him the history of the Mexican Revolution, and the men—Zapata, Madero, and Villa—who shaped Mexican revolutionary thought.

He told her that Cuban liberator, José Martí, had spent considerable time in the Yucatán and was enamored with the Maya civilization. She told him there were plans to dedicate a library in his honor at the Park of the Americas uptown.

When the bus stopped in Piste, near the Maya ceremonial center of Chichén Itzá, they disembarked to stretch their legs. They shared sandwiches and soft drinks. They then boarded the bus and continued in their conversation for several more hours.

When the bus arrived in Mérida, she told him she lived on Calle 61 in the city's historic center near the zoological park. He told her he would be staying at the Hotel Reforma on Calle 59. He asked if he could have her telephone number. She consented. He wrote her telephone number on a box of matches and he invited her out on a date.

She said she would be delighted and that he could come by that evening.

He arrived at her family's home at 9 PM. She answered the door, ready to continue their conversation about history and philosophy. Accompanied by her mother, Socorro Blum de Cámara, the young couple went out for dinner.

In 1955, the Tulipanes was one of the most popular places in Mérdia. It was a restaurant that showcased popular bands and dancing. Alejandro González, like most Latin Americans who parents had emigrated from Galicia, Spain was not a great dancer; Lía had to show him the moves as they danced to the music.

Apart from the music and dancing, they enjoyed venison and she introduced him to regional appetizers that reflected Maya cuisine. In the course of the evening, he confessed he was divorced and had a son. She said she didn't care.

Her mother was impressed with his manners and demeanor. "*Es muy galán*," her mother observed to her daughter, meaning he was very gallant.

As he walked the ladies back home, Lía him what she could offer him to thank him for a wonderful evening. He hesitated, then replied he would accept a chocolate.

"I've been told that chocolate is originally from Mexico," he told her, smiling.

She replied that he had been told right.

Lía Cámara Blum recounted, decades later, that she knew "something big was going to happen in his life."

She loved his smile, his intellect, and his charming way.

They stopped at a shop where she bought three chocolates. After they reached her family home he thanked her—and her mother—for a lovely evening and left.

The following day, Sunday, he showed up at her home after breakfast. Pedro Cámara Lara answered the door. The Cuban exile asked if he could have permission to take his daughter, with his wife as chaperone, to the port of Progreso.

Don Pedro was impressed by this polite Cuban visitor and agreed.

He intended the trip to be a final reconnaissance of the facilities at the port of Progreso; his being accompanied by two Yucatecan women would be a great cover. He was concerned that Batista's spies, who wanted him dead, were following him.

Lía, for her part, thought they were simply going on a picnic at the beach. Her mother had packed refreshments—and chocolates, remembering the young man's preference for chocolate.

The Cámara Blum family did not appreciate the danger they incurred by being in his company until years later when Batista's secret files were opened and their names were included in secret reports.

They spent that morning and early afternoon driving around the beaches along the Yucatecan coast, from Progreso to Chicxulub. They enjoyed a seafood picnic near Progreso's beachfront *malecón*, returning to Mérida in time for Lía to catch the late afternoon bus to Tizimín. She had to be back at school for Monday morning classes.

Alejandro González made a good impression on the family. He would drop by the Cámara Blum household whenever he was in Mérida.

He and don Pedro became friends. Alejandro González admired Mexico and the Mexican Revolution, he would tell Lía's father. Decades later, Fidel Castro would write: "Mexico was a country that had carried out a great revolution in the second decade of the twentieth century, a revolution that had a lot of prestige and left behind a lot of progressive thinking and a stable government. Every other nation in the region was ruled by tyrants."

Ridding Cuba of a tyrant, Fulgencio Batista, would be the purpose of his return to Cuba once his preparations were finalized. Don Pedro dismissed such talk as nonsense, the exuberance of a youthful dreamer. He believed the young man, so enamored of his daughter, was a "crazy idealist"—and advised him against wanting to change the world.

Socorro Blum de Cámara, for her part, tried to change the topics of conversation away from politics whenever the discussions became animated or heated. She would offer coffee and talk to Alejandro about life and love.

Amid smiles and friendship, and a growing love for Lía, Alejandro González felt at home in the company of this Mexican family that came to embrace him as a son.

In Mérida Alejandro fell in love with Lía. As lovers have always done, they would go out to dinner, have ice cream in the park, see movies at the Cinema Mérida, and enjoy chocolates at the cafés.

He loved Mérida, he told her, because it reminded him of Havana. He was right: *Before Night Falls* was filmed in Mérida in 1992, the city passing for Havana of the 1960s. He loved walking its streets, meandering through the Historic Center.

The lovers would stroll from Mejorada Park to the Church of Santiago. He marveled at the twin houses Mérida's first chocolatier had built for his daughters on Calle 59 between 72nd and 74th Streets.

They visited the port of Progreso several more times. Lía and Socorro both accompanied him to the ruins of Chichén Itzá where he climbed the Castillo pyramid.

But it was in the darkened Cine Mérida movie house that he declared his love for her. Lía told him she was in love with him as well.

They kissed.

He told her his love was true.

But he also told her his love for his country was equally strong—and so was his commitment to securing his nation's freedom. Alejandro told Lía he had obligations to take care of first, his love for her notwithstanding: He would have to leave Mexico, but he would send for her.

When she asked why he had to leave, he quoted José Martí: "We light the oven so that everyone may bake bread in it."

She smiled and said little more. He promised again he would send for her.

Lía was stoic. She was also aware that he was busy, meeting with other Cuban exiles, befriending other Yucatecan families.

It would not be until he overthrew Fulgencio Batista, months after he returned to Cuba—and his photograph was flashed in headlines around the world—that Lía learned Alejandro González's true name: *Fidel Alejandro Castro Ruz*.

Fidel Alejandro Castro Ruz broke Lía Cámara Blum's heart.

Months of silence between the lovers followed.

Not until he consolidated power in Cuba, did he send Lía a note inviting her to travel to Havana.

It was a thrilling prospect. Her parents, however, counselled her to be prudent.

She arrived in Cuba in 1960 for the *Encuentro de Juventud Latinoamericana*, or the Latin American Youth Summit. She was welcomed as a "revolutionary" and she traveled throughout the island as a dignitary. On at least one occasion Ernesto "Che" Guevara introduced her as the future First Lady of Cuba.

All the while, however, she knew her parents were right, especially as the *Revolucion* began to take a more sinister, authoritarian turn.

Lía could not be part of Fidel's Revolution; she could not stand the possibility of a public life in a foreign country next to man whose heart she loved but whose thinking she no longer trusted or understood.

Had he forgotten everything she taught him about the principles of the Mexican Revolution?

"I cannot be your Eva," she told Fidel, a reference to Eva Perón, the loyal wife to Argentine dictator, Juan Perón. "I cannot stay with you in Cuba," she said. She also quoted José Martí: "A selfish man is a thief."

She kissed Fidel Castro one final time.

It was now Lía's turn to break Fidel's heart.

Lía Cámara Blum returned to Mérida. Fidel Castro went on to rule Cuba for decades and she continued with her life in Mérida, marrying a Cuban exile and having two children.

Despite this unexpected turn of events—*el Comandante* was not used to having his offers refused or his heart broken—Fidel's fondness and nostalgia for his time in Mérida remained firm.

In the decades since Lía turned Fidel down, in surreptitious diplomatic pouches, Mexican chocolates have been sent to *el Comandante*, sweet reminders of what lovers break each other's hearts.

You didn't know?

You didn't know that all this time chocolate, clandestinely and secretly, has been sent from Mérida to Havana, an unexpected reminder of Fidel's love affair in the Yucatán?

In the same way that he broke hearts in Mérida, he would go on to break hearts throughout the whole of Cuba, of course. Fidel would break the hearts of millions of his countrymen as completely as he broke Lía's.

Chocolates from Mérida have offered Fidel a consolation. Chocolates from Mérida have served to remind Fidel of the love he left behind.

Mérida.

Where Fidel Castro planned his revolution, where José Martí wrote poems, and where Lía Cámara Blum had her heart broken.

Havana.

Where surreptitious chocolates from Mérida have soothed the broken heart of a lonely revolutionary whose Revolution has come to dust.

Lía Cámara Blum, now a grandmother and a long-retired teacher, remembers the love affair with the Cuban revolutionary. She lives in the same house where "Alejandro González" came by to pick her up on their first date. "This is where he stood when he met my parents for the first time," she says.

"Had he stayed in Mérida," Socorro Blum de Cámara once remarked during the Cuban Missile Crisis, "everyone would have been better off."

Had he stayed in Mérida, in other words, the world would know fewer broken hearts.

Alas.

Hearts are broken every day.

The magnificent photographs in this book capture the lives of a people whose hearts are broken every day.

Louis E.V. Nevaer
Mérida, Yucatán

Cuba Beckons

As soon as President Obama announced, on December 16, 2014, that his administration would lift travel restrictions to Cuba, I started to look for available flights to Havana. I found one from Montreal direct to Havana, but ultimately chose to fly first to Grand Cayman, and from there to Cuba.

I couldn't wait.

A little background about me. I was born in Key West, Florida, a mere 93 miles from Havana. My father served in the Navy, during the Cuban Missile Crisis in 1962. He was stationed on an aircraft carrier off the coast of Cuba.

Tensions between the countries resulted in a trade embargo, which included a ban on all leisure travel to the Communist country.

Cuba has, from that moment, been the forbidden island that Americans were not allowed to visit—until now.

Prior to President Obama's brave decision to turn a new page, it was almost impossible for individual Americans to visit Cuba. Indeed, in 2014 I tried to get permission from the Treasury Department to travel to Cuba. My request was denied. The reason? I had failed to list exactly where I would be day to day in Havana.

My interest in Cuba has to do with more than having been born in Key West and my father having served during the Cuban Missile Crisis. My best friend from college, Raúl Rubiera, was Cuban. His family was forced into exile. They left Cuba after Fidel Castro declared the *revolución communista* and began to seize all private property.

Sitting up late at night in our dorm rooms, Raúl told me many stories of Cuba.

I was fascinated. I was intrigued. I knew I had to go one day.

Fast-forward a few decades.

I became a photographer. I lived in the Hudson Valley, in the town of Saugerties to be precise.

And when the opportunity to travel to Cuba arose, I seized it.

Cuba and the Cubans

The size of the city of Havana took me by surprise. If it were located in the United States, it would be our fourth largest city, about the size of Chicago.

When I arrived, I was excited to see everything and to talk to everyone I could. I should say that, in the process, I destroyed the Spanish language, but the Cubans hung in there with me.

They are a vibrant, joyful people, and I thoroughly enjoyed being in their company. They have a lot of energy. Cubans have a remarkable resilience, evident in how they manage to find a way to fix everything, from broken-down cars to getting a deal on a box of cigars.

Of course, they have to fix everything because there are few shops, and everything needs repair. The only exceptions are the meager offerings in hotel lobby shops and designated tourist stores. Otherwise, there are no car lots, no appliance stores, and no hardware stores.

When I met with Rolando Mesa, Professor of Spanish at the University of Havana, he told me, "We have no Internet, we don't know what is going on. We just want to know what is happening in the outside world."

He said this to me over a glass of *canchánchara*, a rum drink with honey and lime, at a hard-currency café, one of the new establishments that the government allows private citizens to run.

The Cuban people I met are eager—desperate—for the embargo to be lifted. They are also leery of the possibility of corporate America "invading" the island. They still have memories of their economy being dominated by American corporations and of theMafia corrupting Cuba's sociopolitical life.

An indication of the fatigue with the *revolución* is seen in the Ladies in White (Damas de Blanco, *www.damasdeblanco.com*), a group of women who hold protest marches every Sunday along Fifth Avenue (Quinta Avenida) in the Miramar neighborhood. They assemble in front of Santa Rita Church and lobby for the right of free speech and for civil liberties++. Two Sundays before I photographed a march, 52 of the ladies were arrested. Most members are women whose husbands, sons, brothers, or uncles have been arrested for speaking out against the government and are serving long prison terms for being "antisocial" and "antirevolutionary" dissenters.

The march that I photographed was also being videotaped by the authorities; to intimidate the Cuban public, four cameras recorded everyone nearby, including spectators.

Fidel and Raúl Castro are in their final years. And as much as this brings hope of new freedoms, the Cubans are apprehensive of what will happen next.

Will the embargo be lifted?

Will Guantánamo be returned to Cuba?

Will opposition parties be legalized?

Will the Cuban Communist Party be dismantled?

Is there a promising future the Cuban nation?

Visiting Cuba

Going to Cuba is not a vacation in any sense of what most Americans think a Caribbean vacation should be. Going to Cuba is an exotic adventure.

Yes, you could spend the entire time at the Hotel Nacional, travel everywhere by taxi, eat only at the government-operated restaurants, or travel on a tour bus with other international tourists.

But if you do that, you will miss the best part of going to Cuba: reaching out to the Cuban people.

It's all in what we want to see. I have tried to take photographs that make you want to see as much as you can of the beautiful island of Cuba and her wonderful people.

Michael Nelson

Saugerties, New York
July 2016

Havana

Havana begins preparations for Barack Obama's historic visit to the island nation

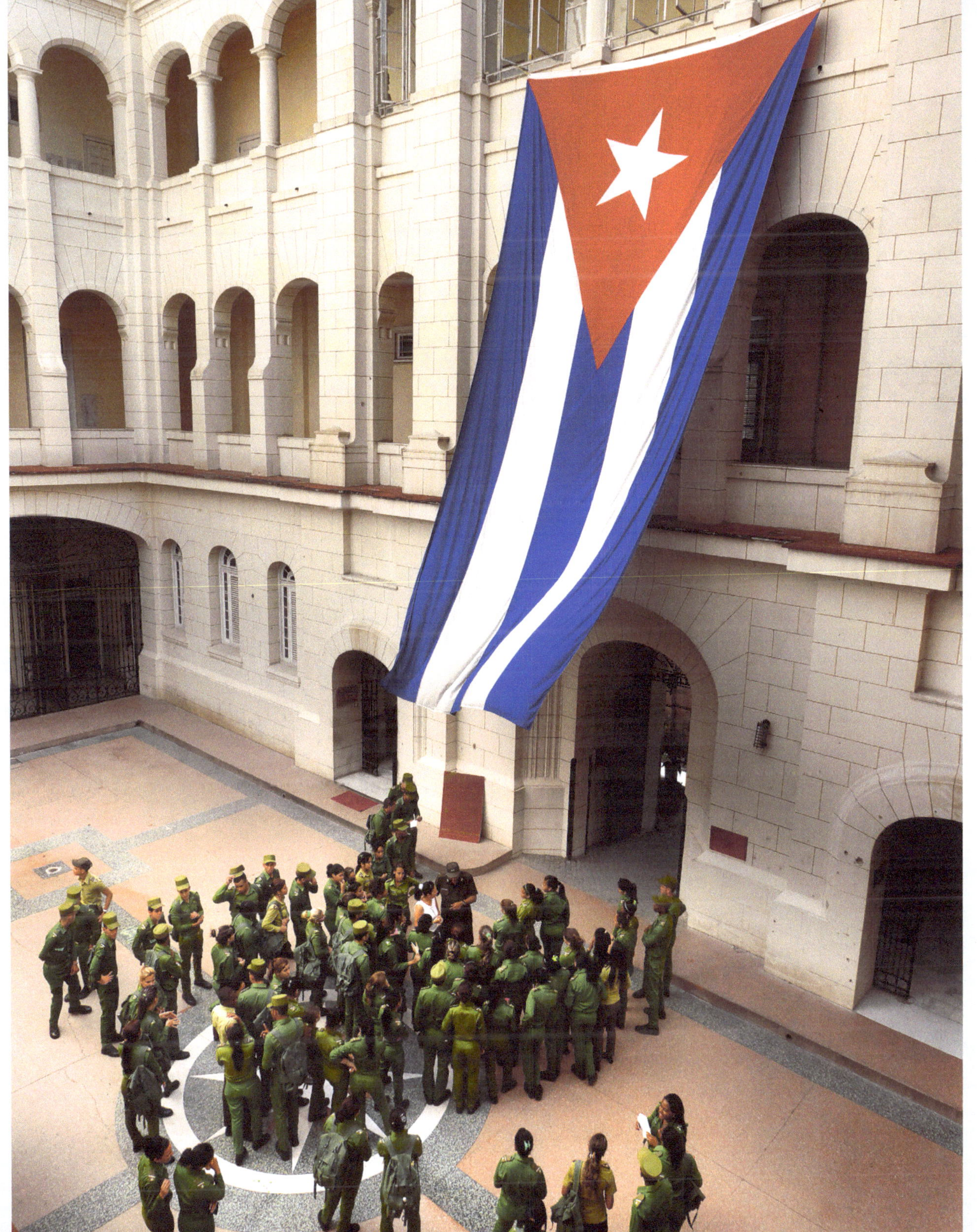

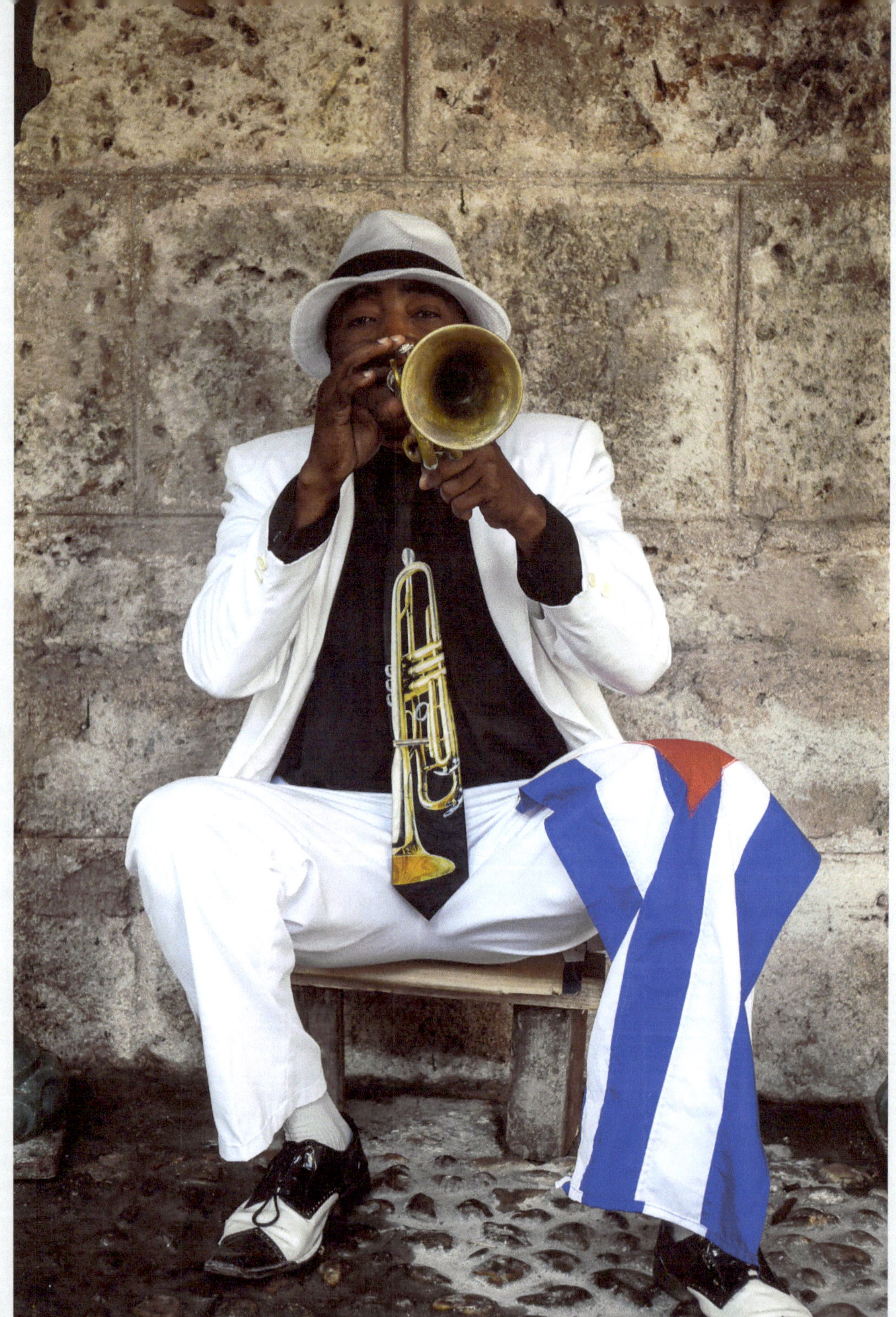

A dapper musician playing for tips in Old Havana

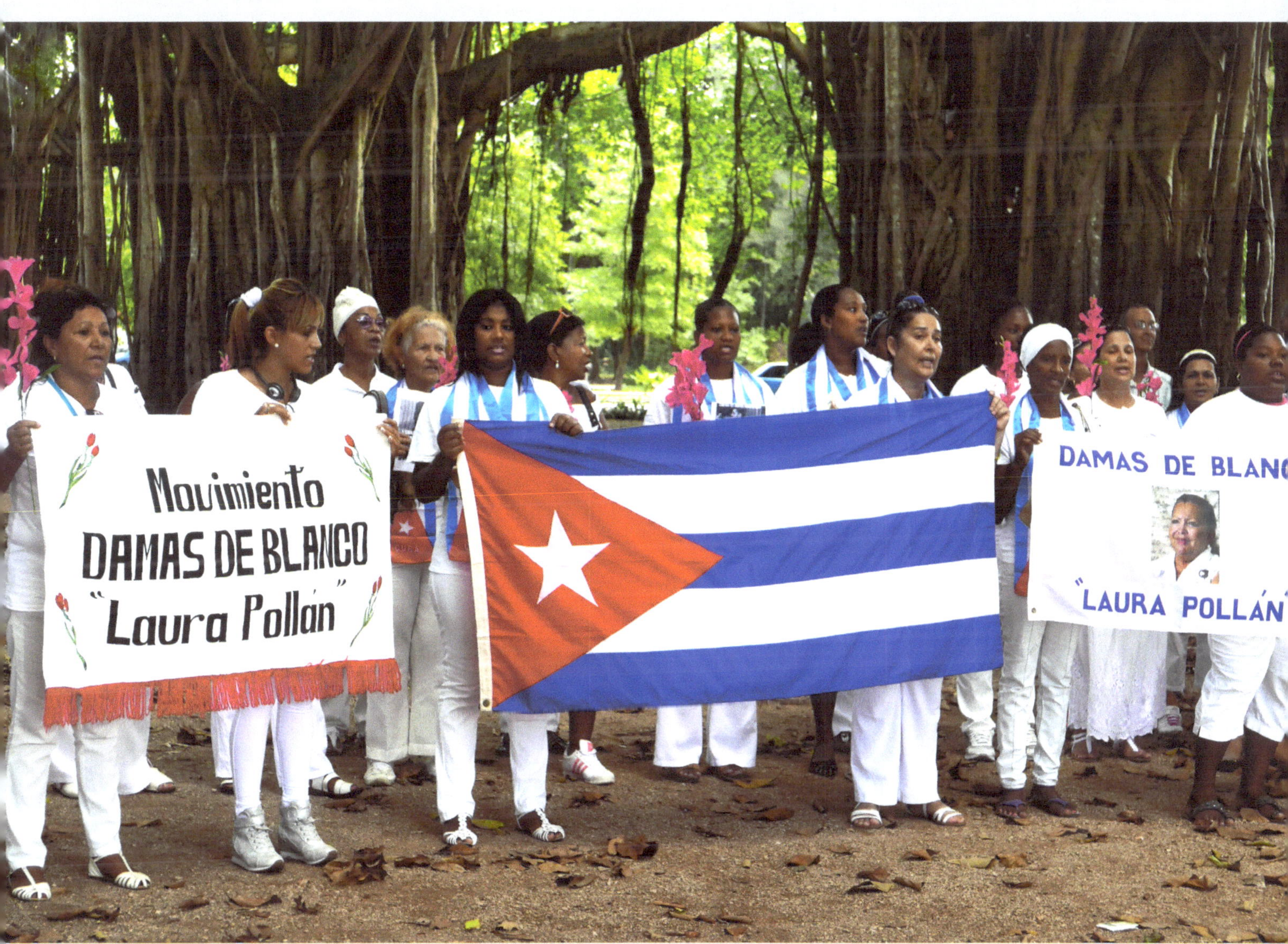

The Ladies in White political activists seeking civil liberties

The Ladies in White on their weekly "March in Silence" in the Miramar neighborhood

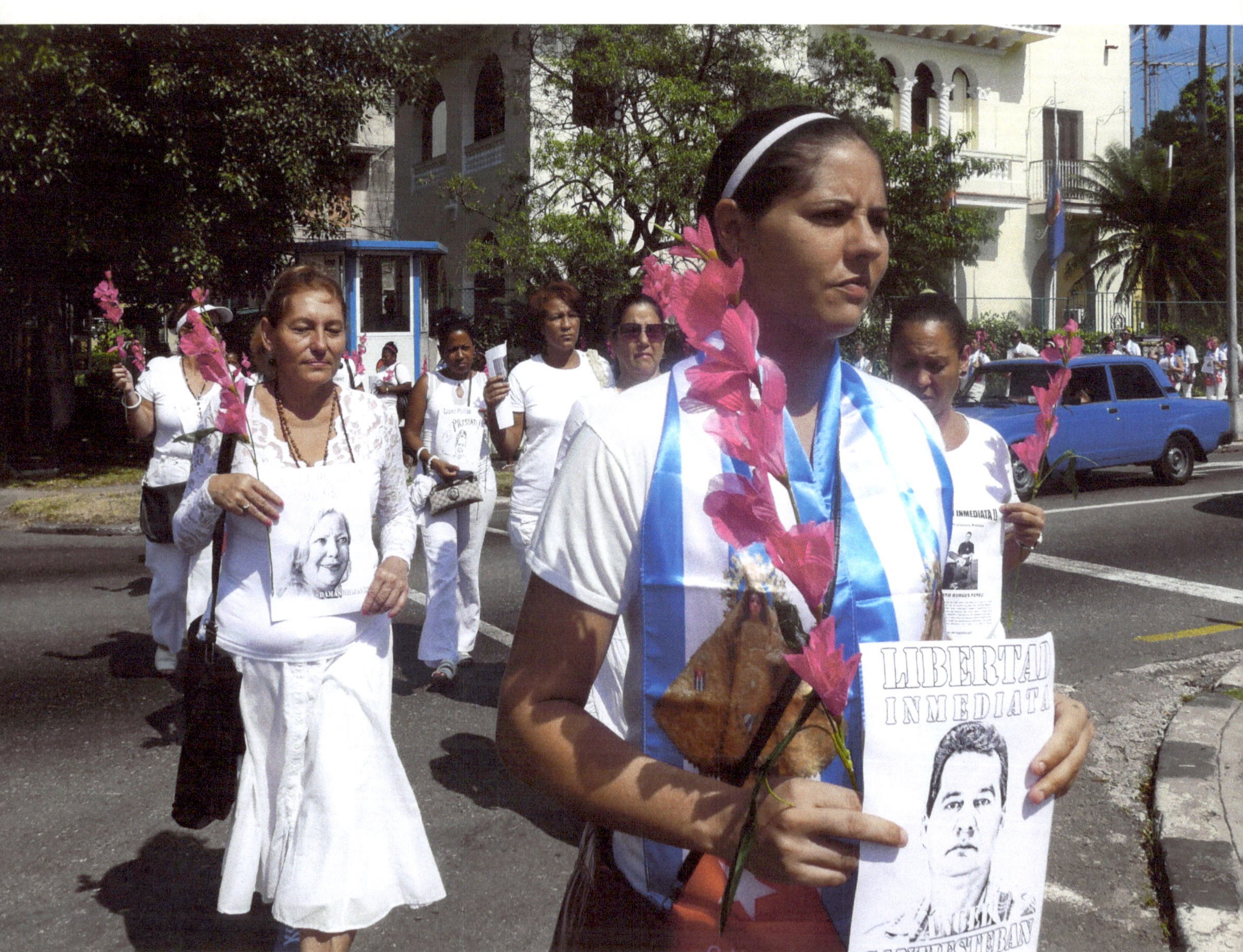

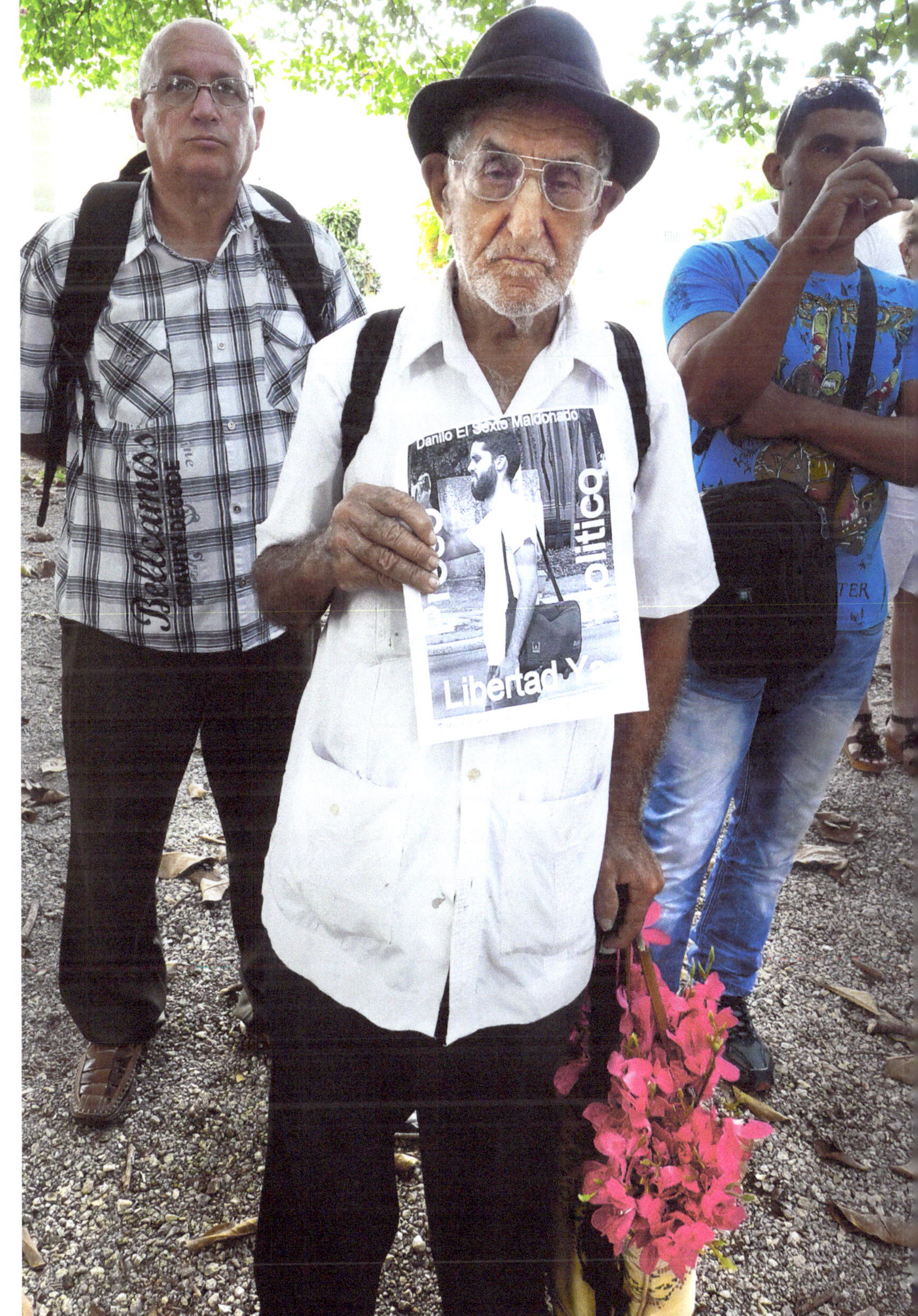

An elderly man bearing witness to the unlawful detention of his dissident son

Love always finds a way

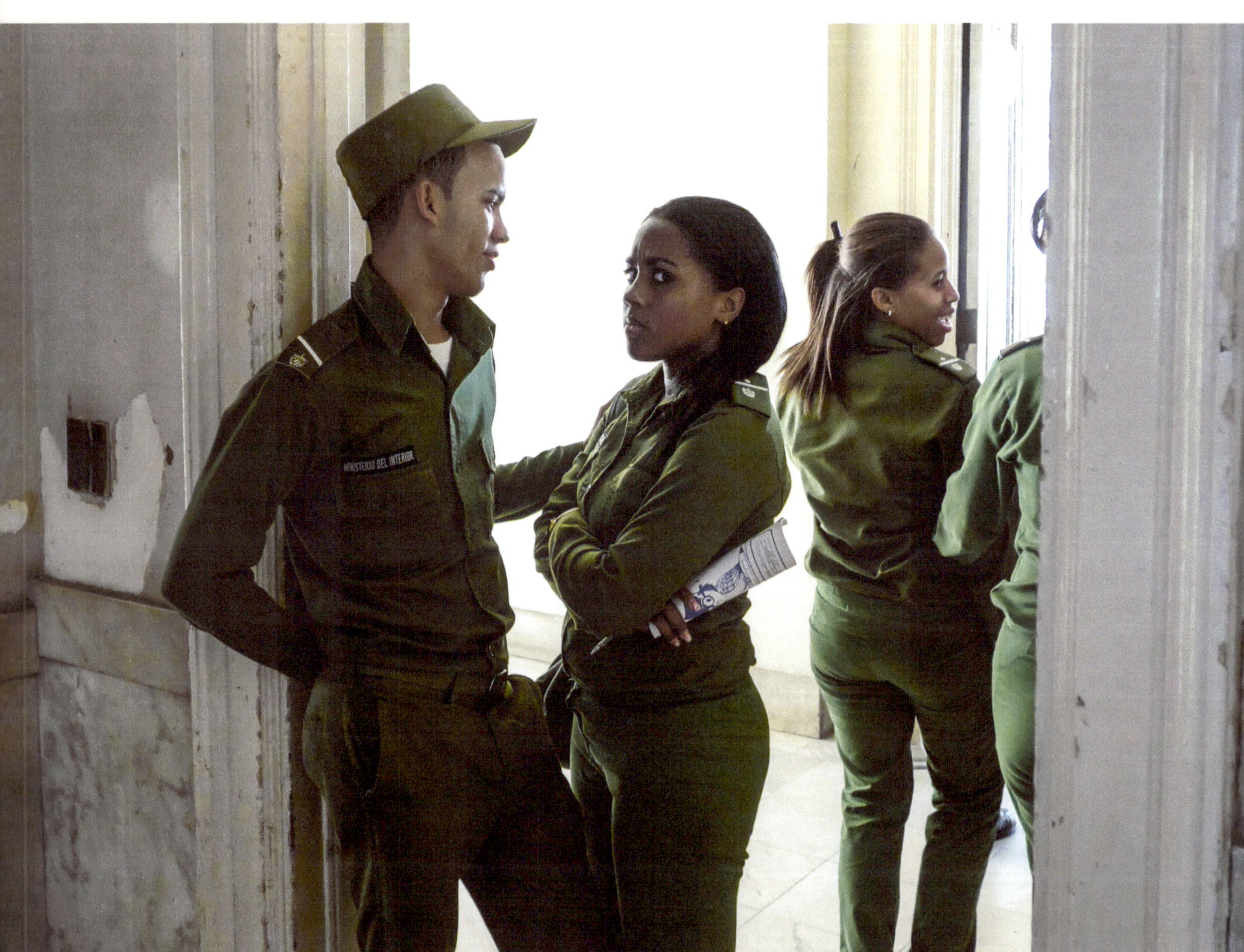

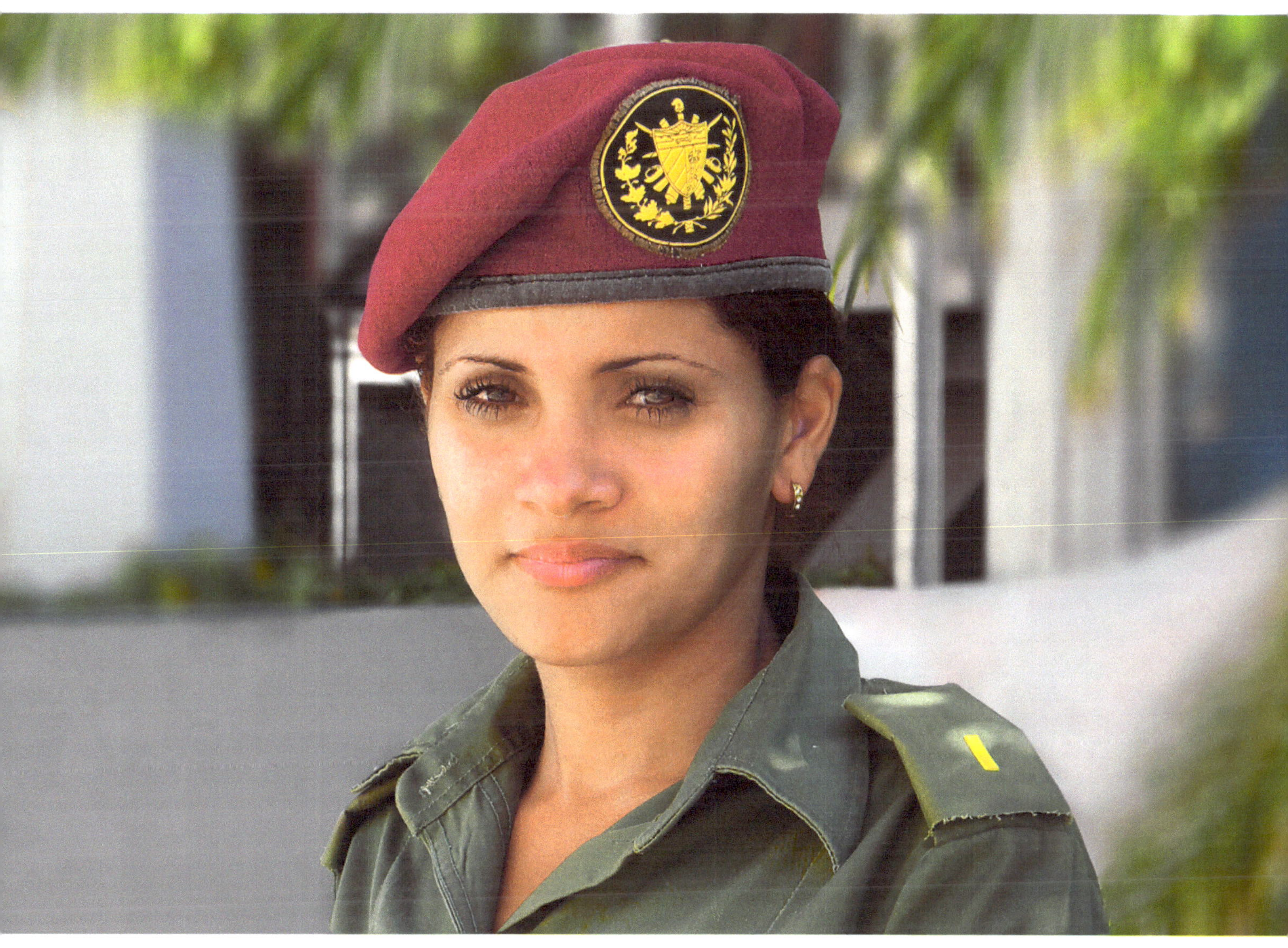

"I Can always find my Cuban skies in Rosalinda's eyes"

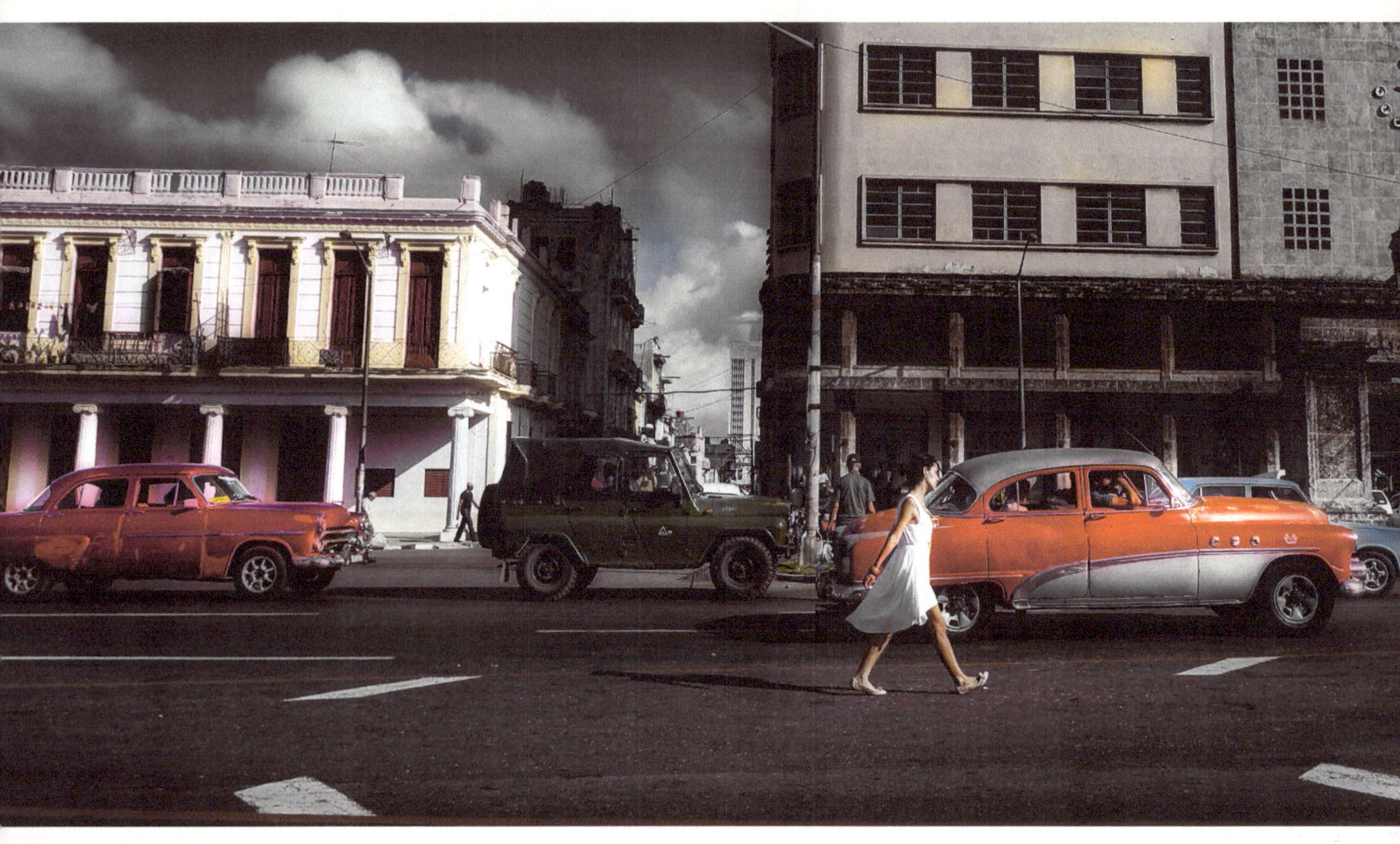

Central Havana

Unloved and in disrepair, both its architecture and her people

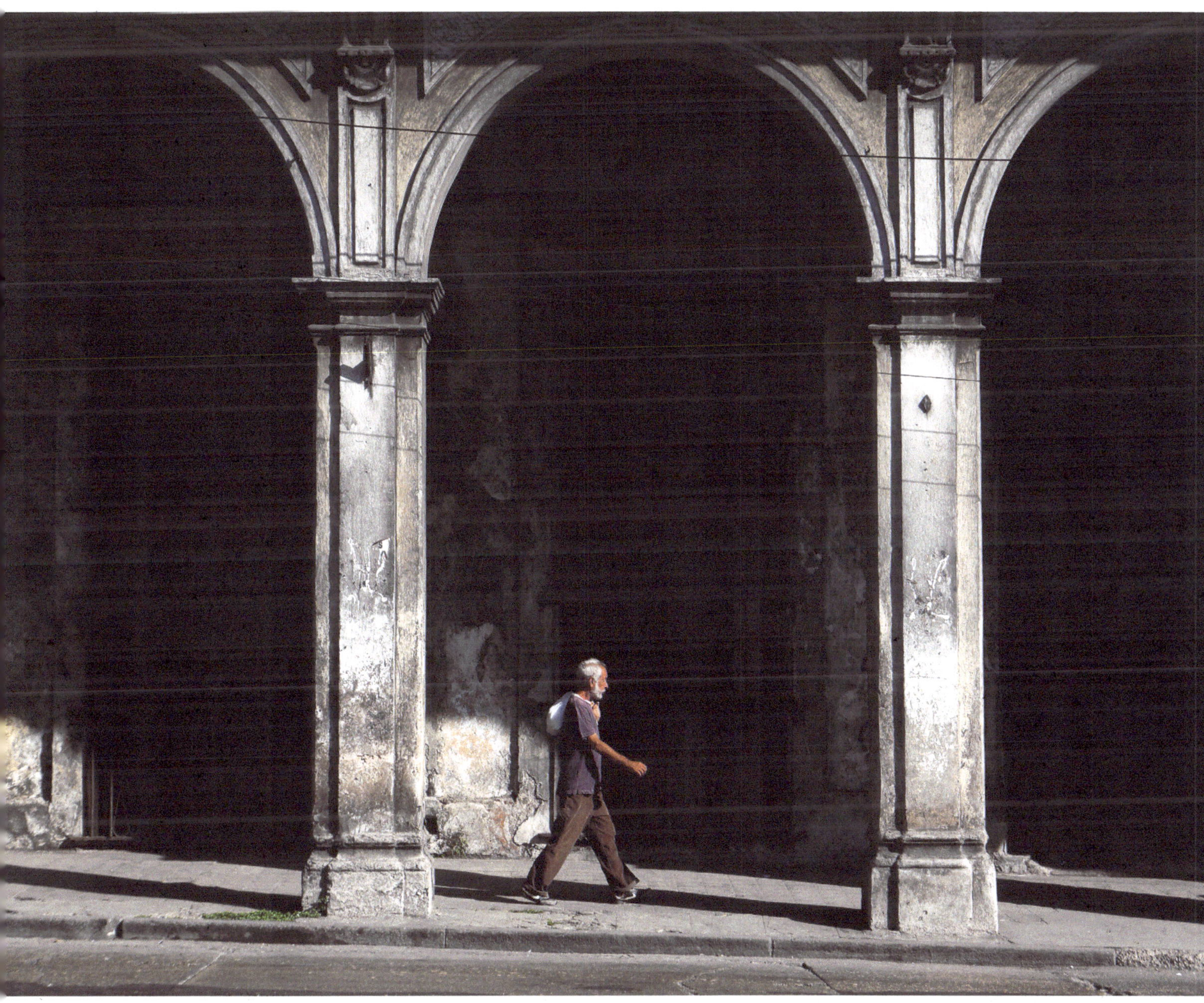

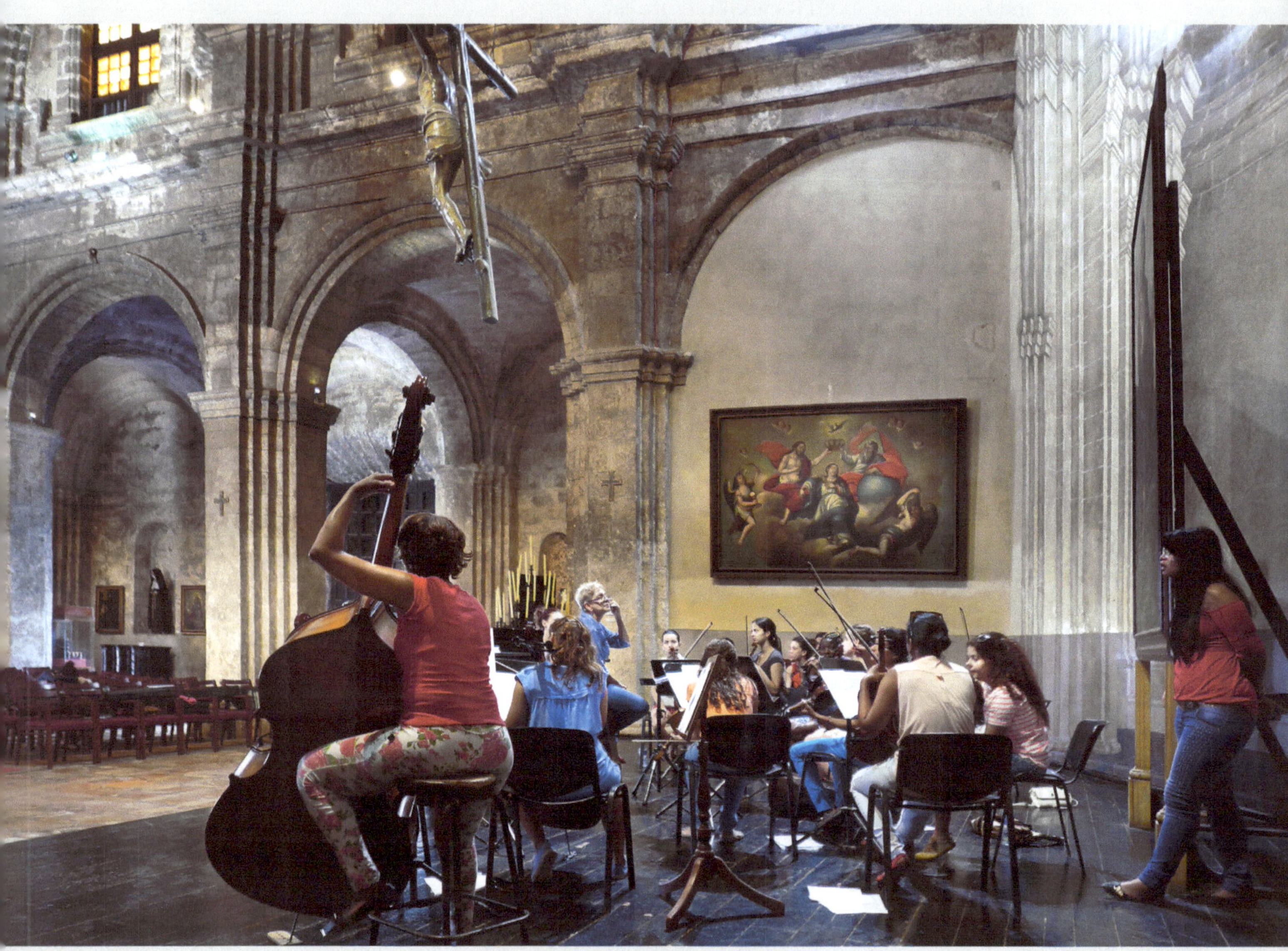

A musical interlude in Havana's cathedral

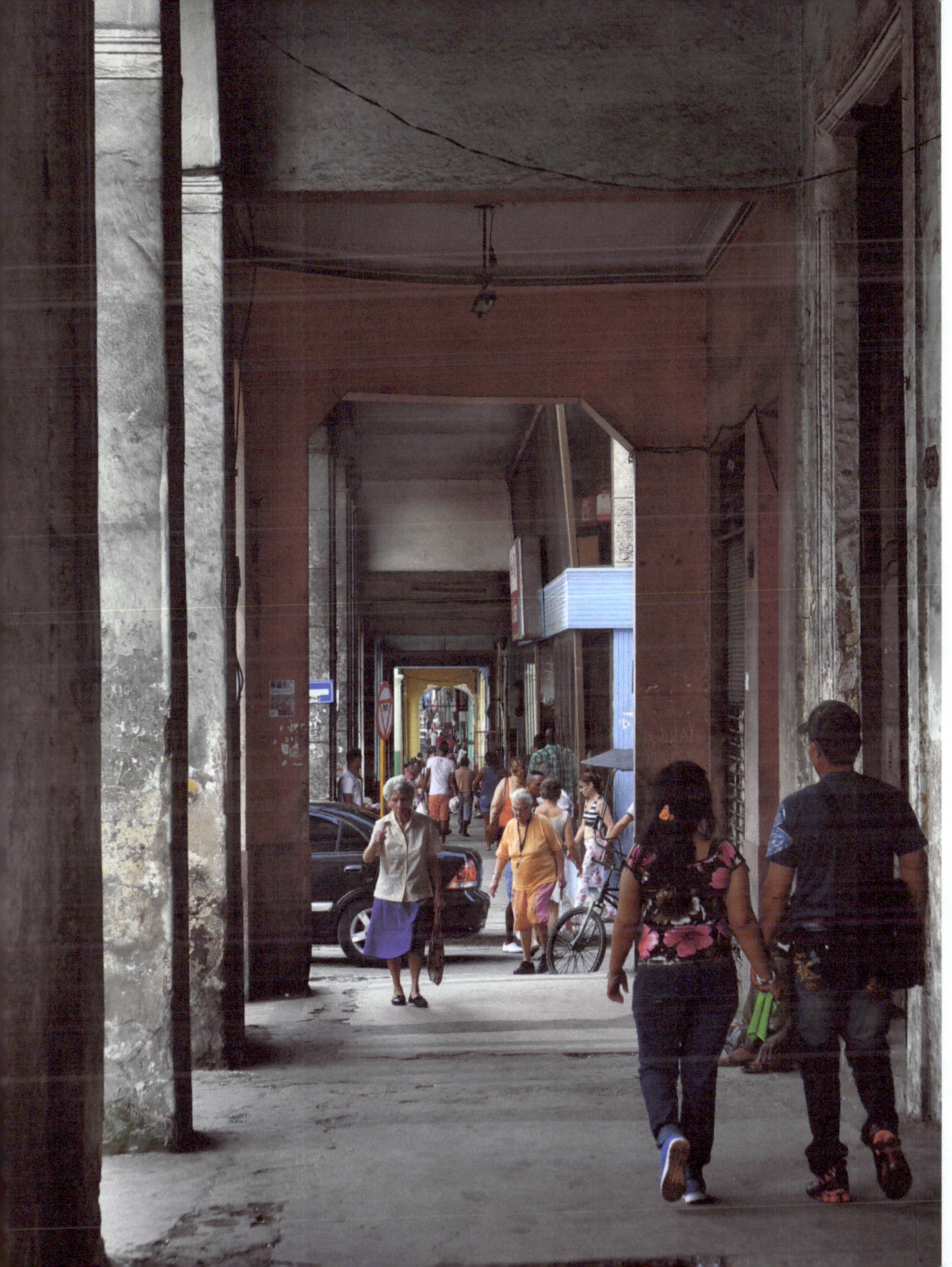

Pedestrians about their daily lives, Central Havana

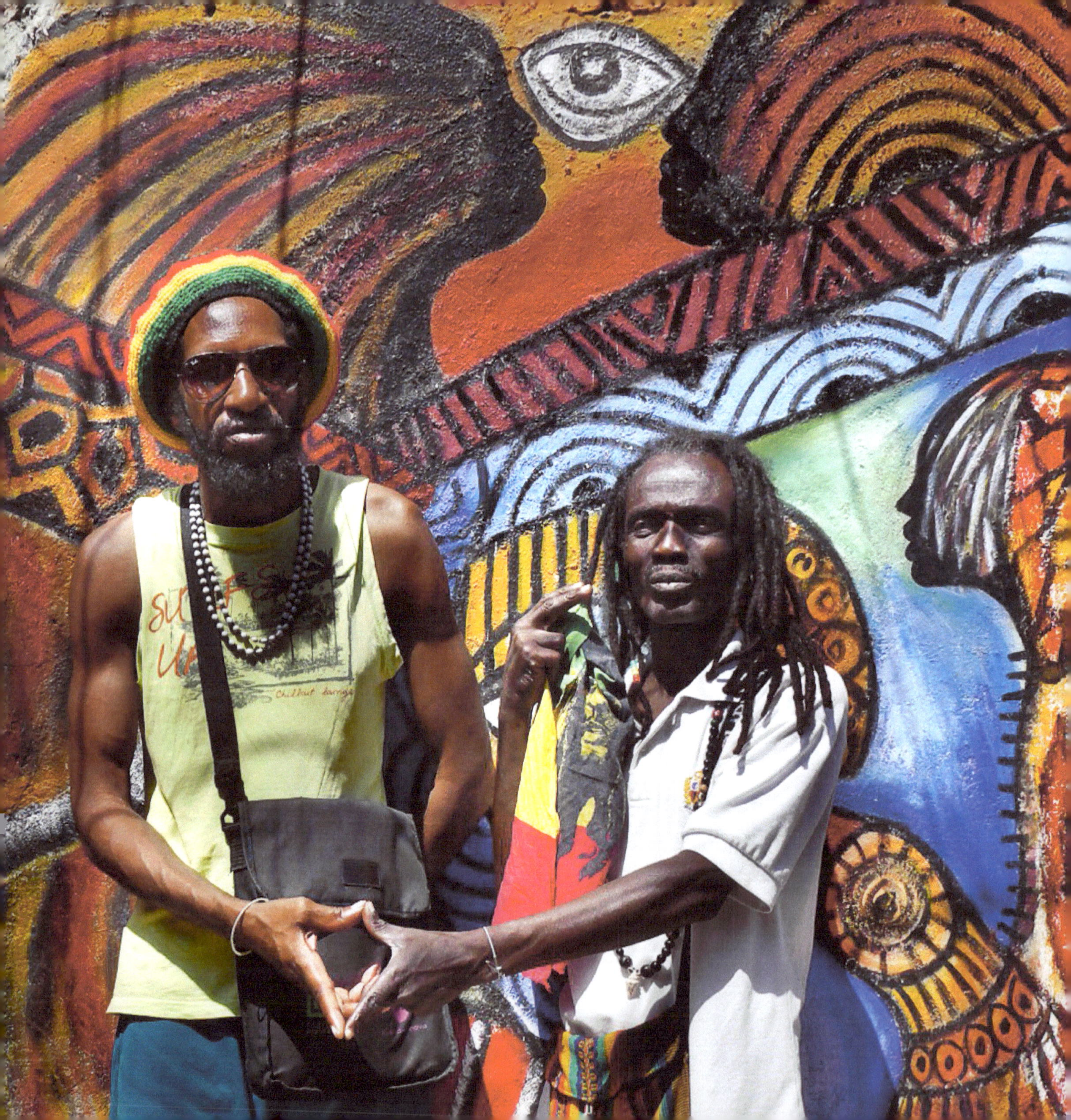

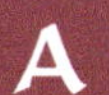

A bold affirmation of Cuba's African heritage and culture

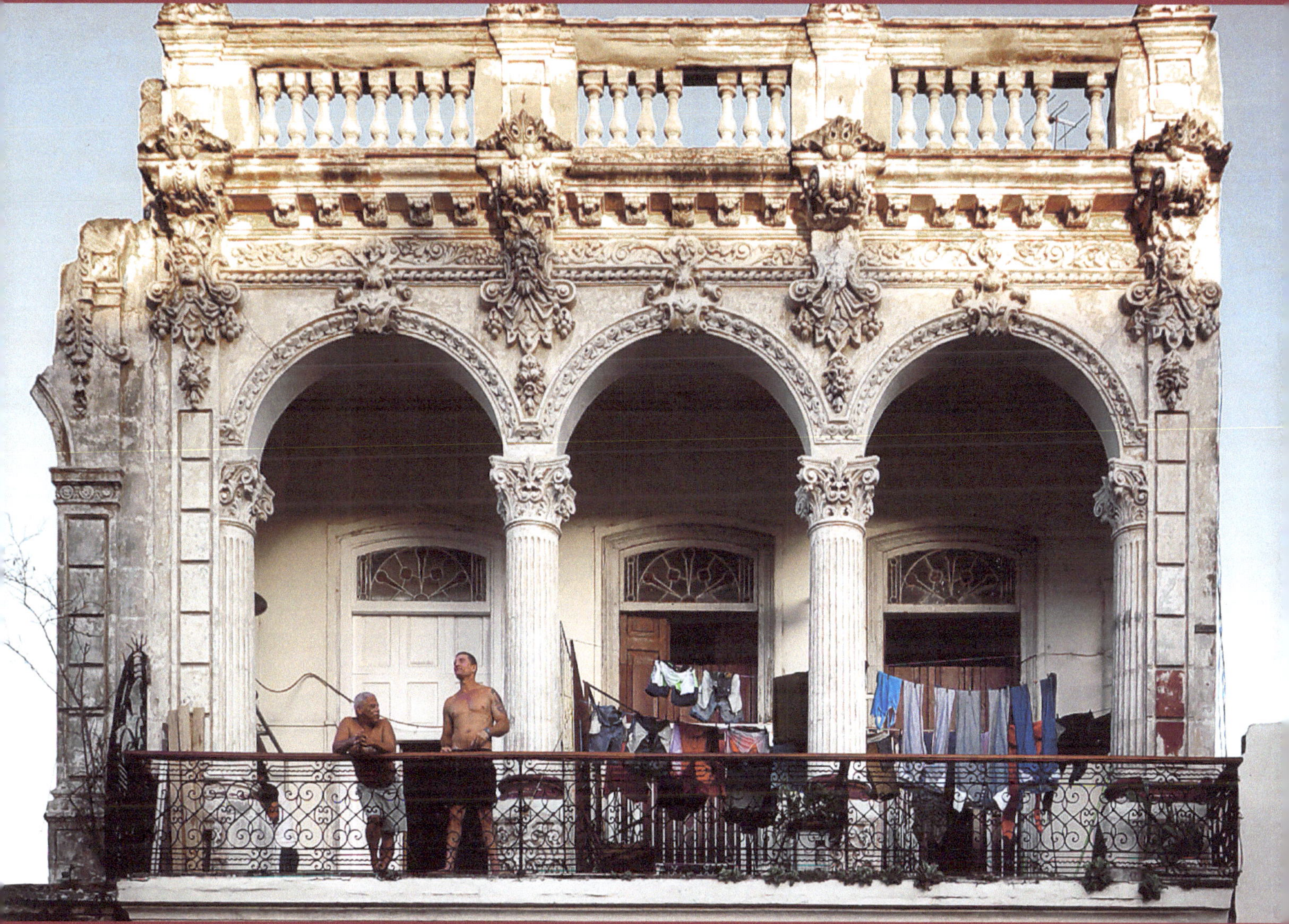

Life among the ruins of the Vedado neighborhood

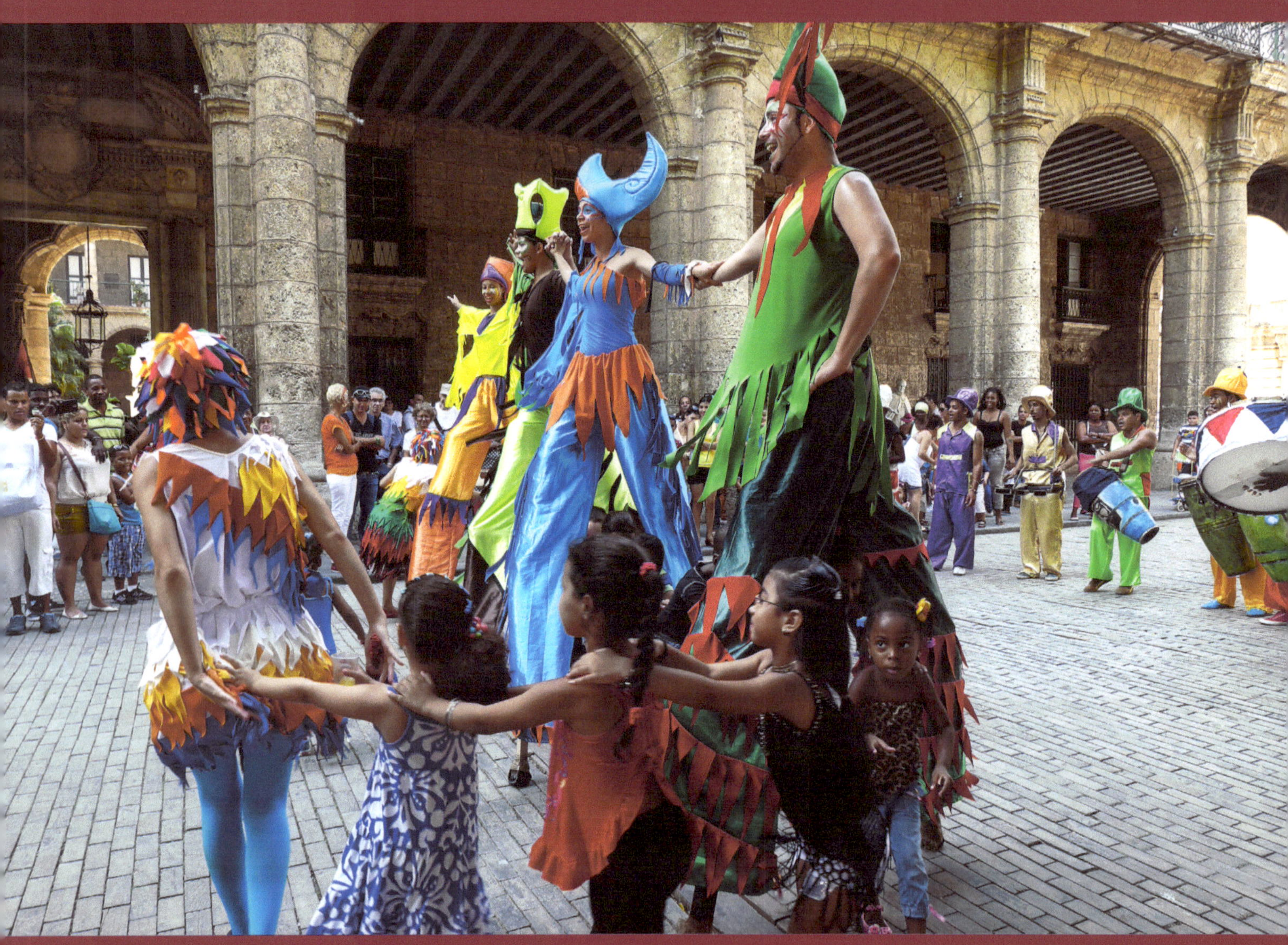

Spectacle and merriment for visitors in Old Havana

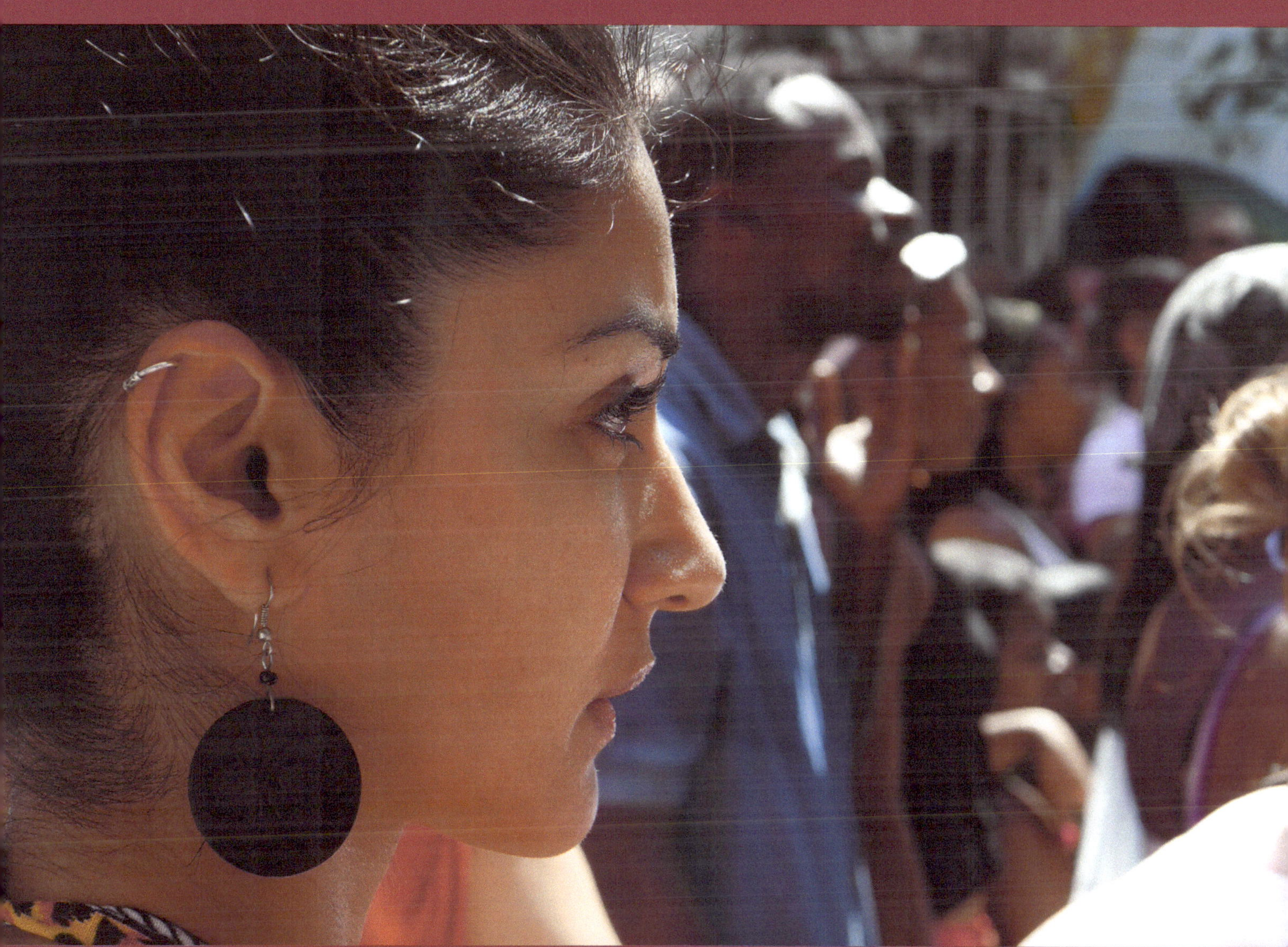

Cuban beauty with round earring

Taxi in search of a fare, Central Havana

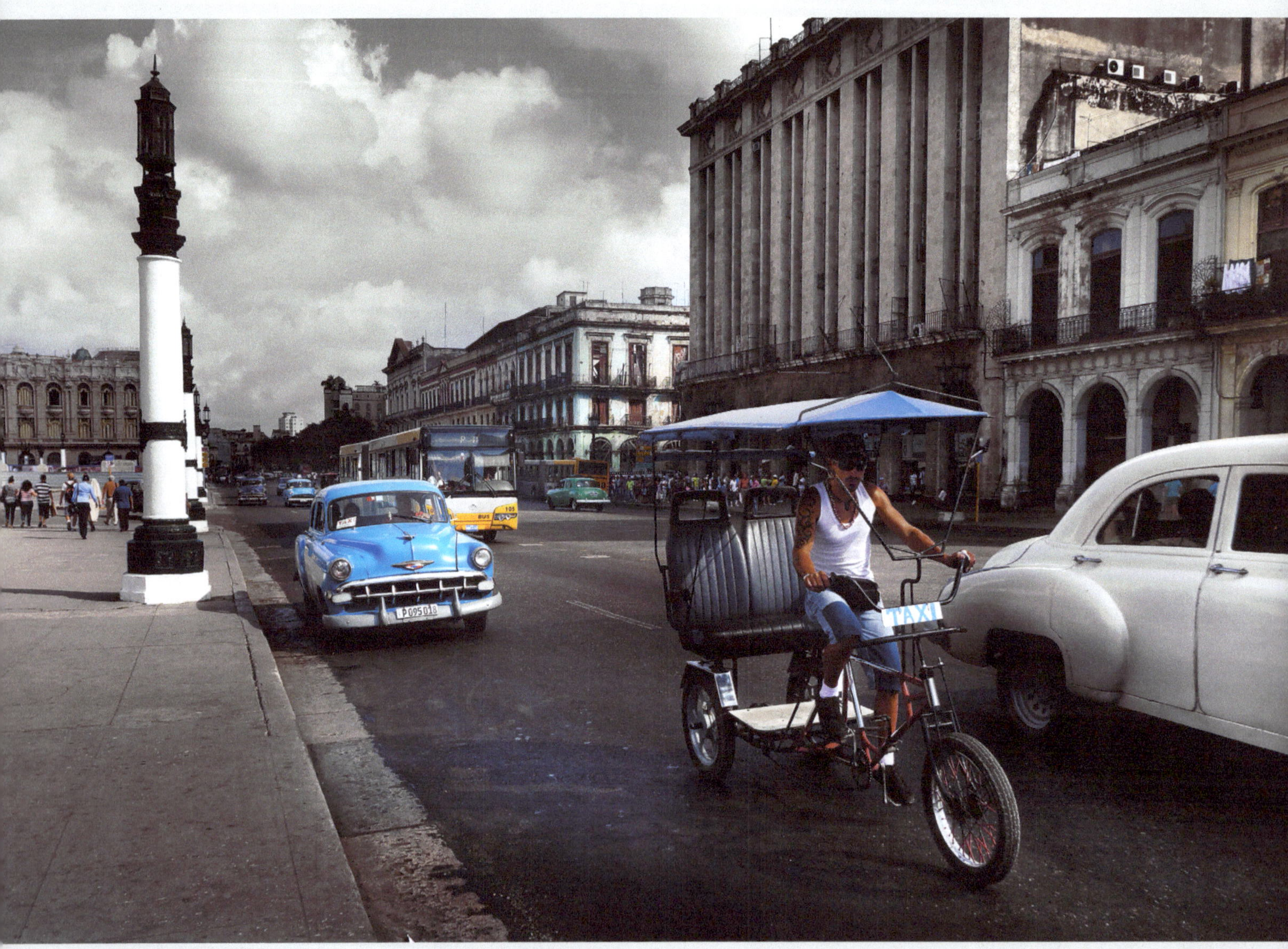

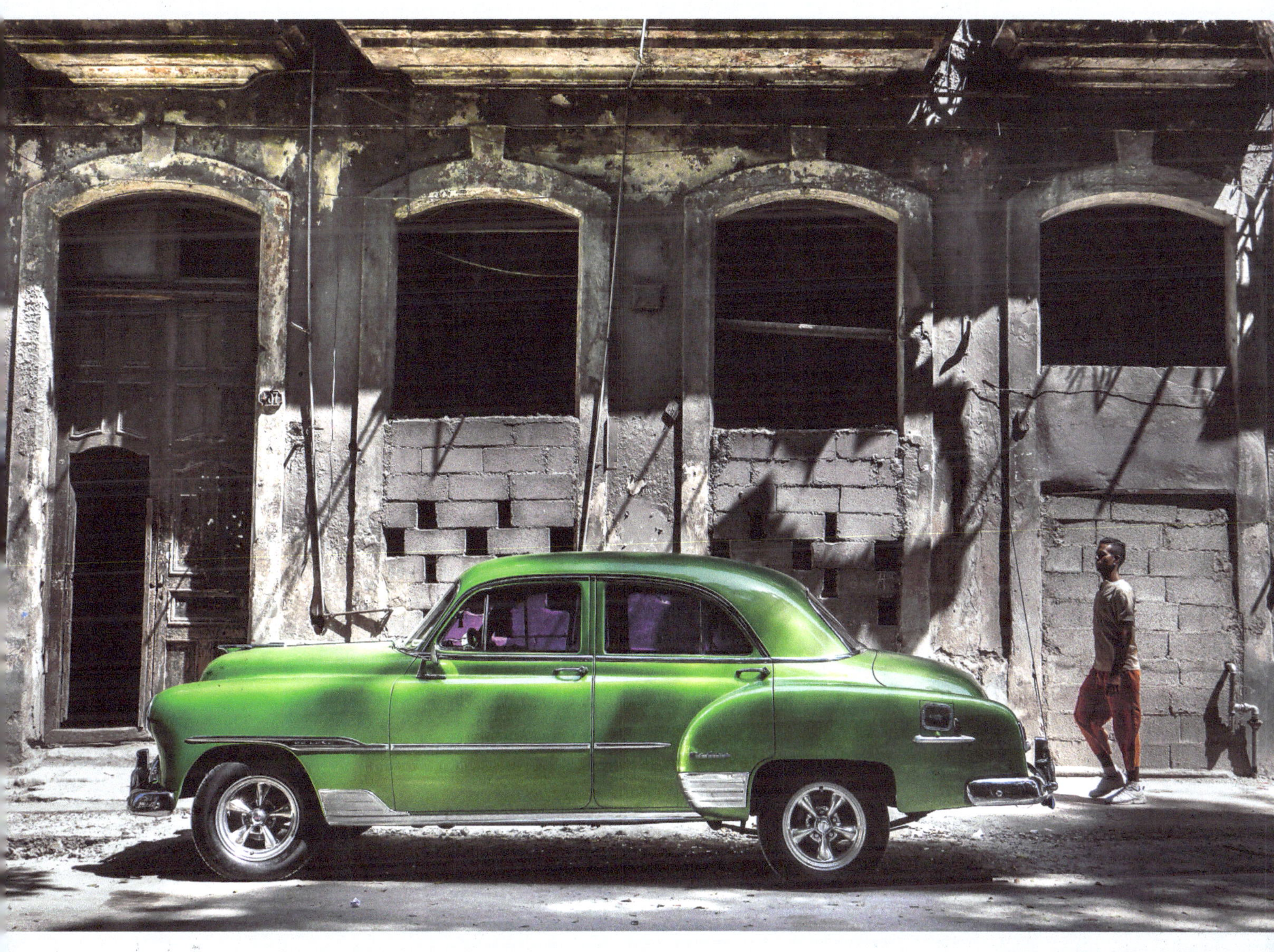

Vintage American car on a side street, Central Havana

Vintage American cars driving past the Great Theatre of Havana Alicia Alonso

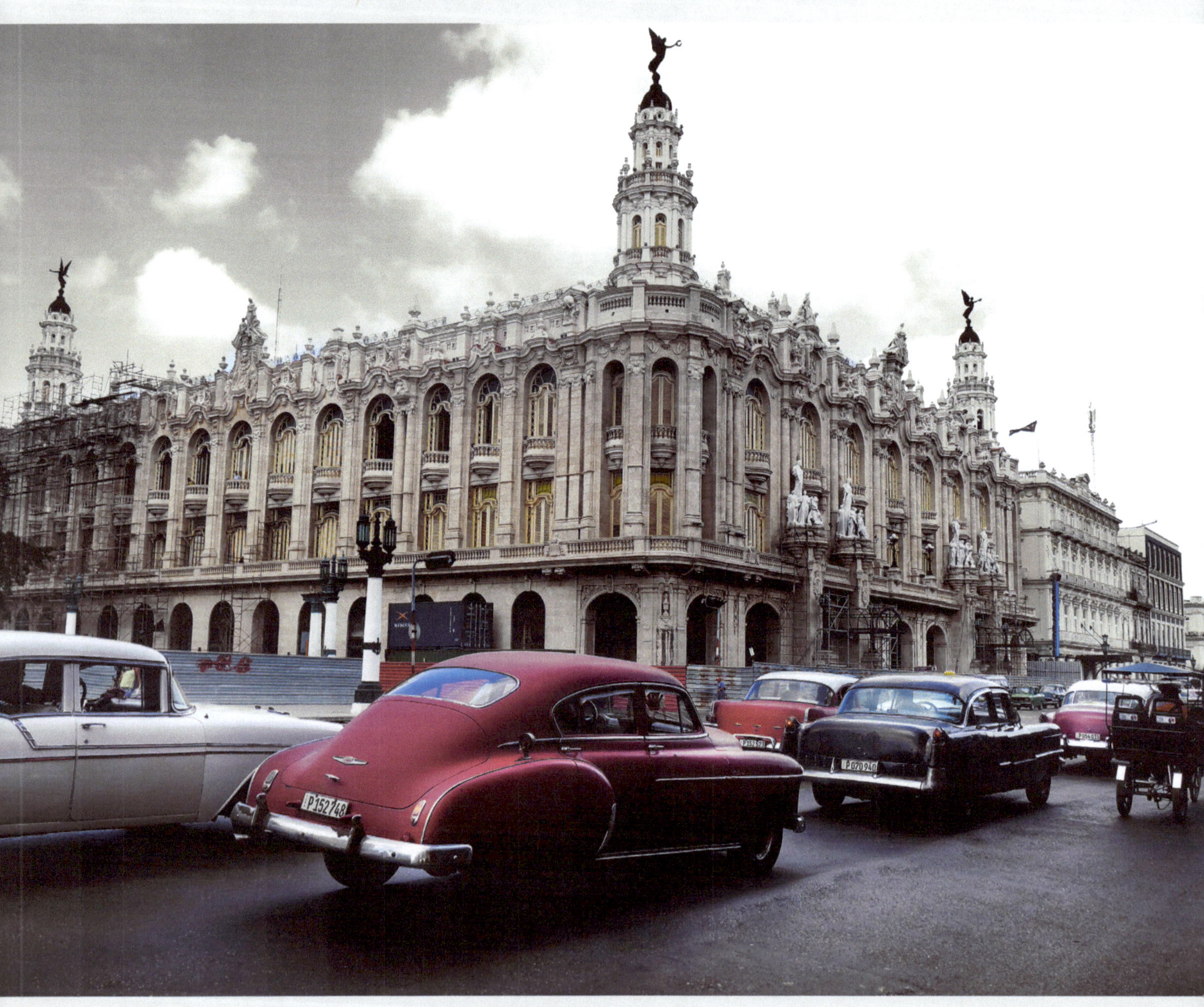

The Floridita bar, made famous by Ernest Hemingway, where the daiquiri is believed to have been invented

▶

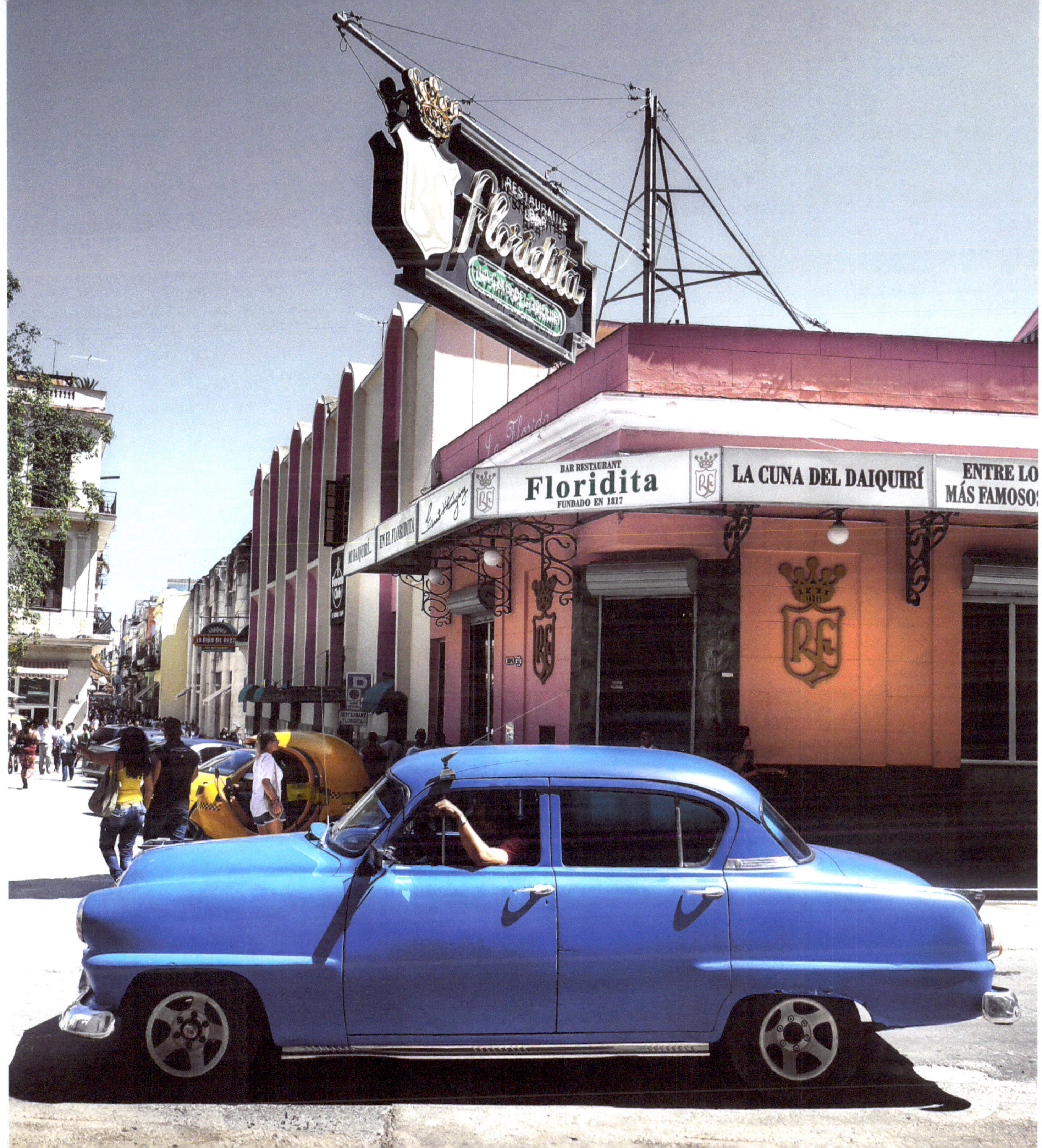
Floridita
BAR RESTAURANT
Floridita
FUNDADO EN 1817
LA CUNA DEL DAIQUIRÍ
ENTRE LO
MÁS FAMOSOS
EN EL FLORIDITA

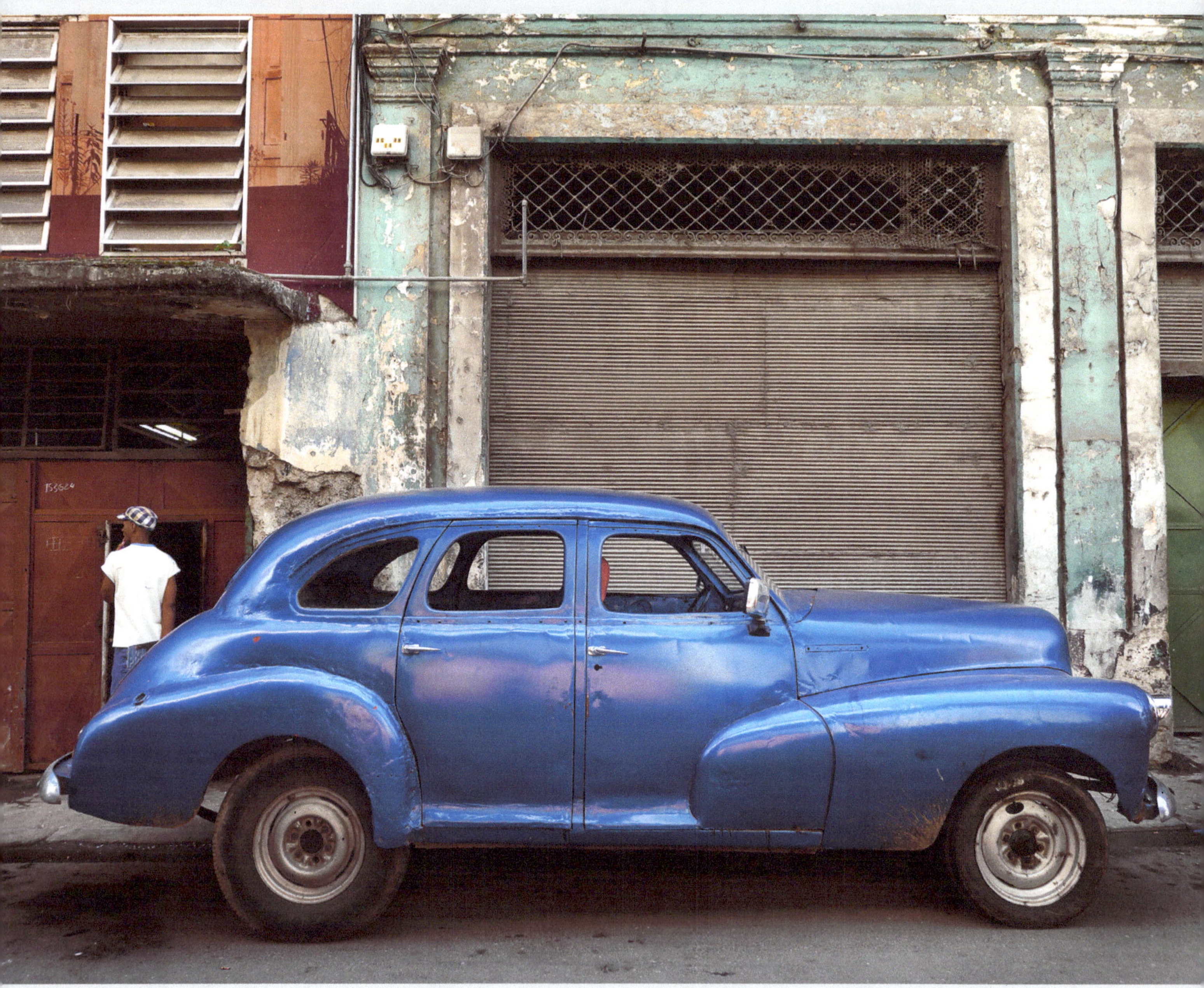

Vintage American car on a side street near the Vedado neighborhood

City scene in Central Havana

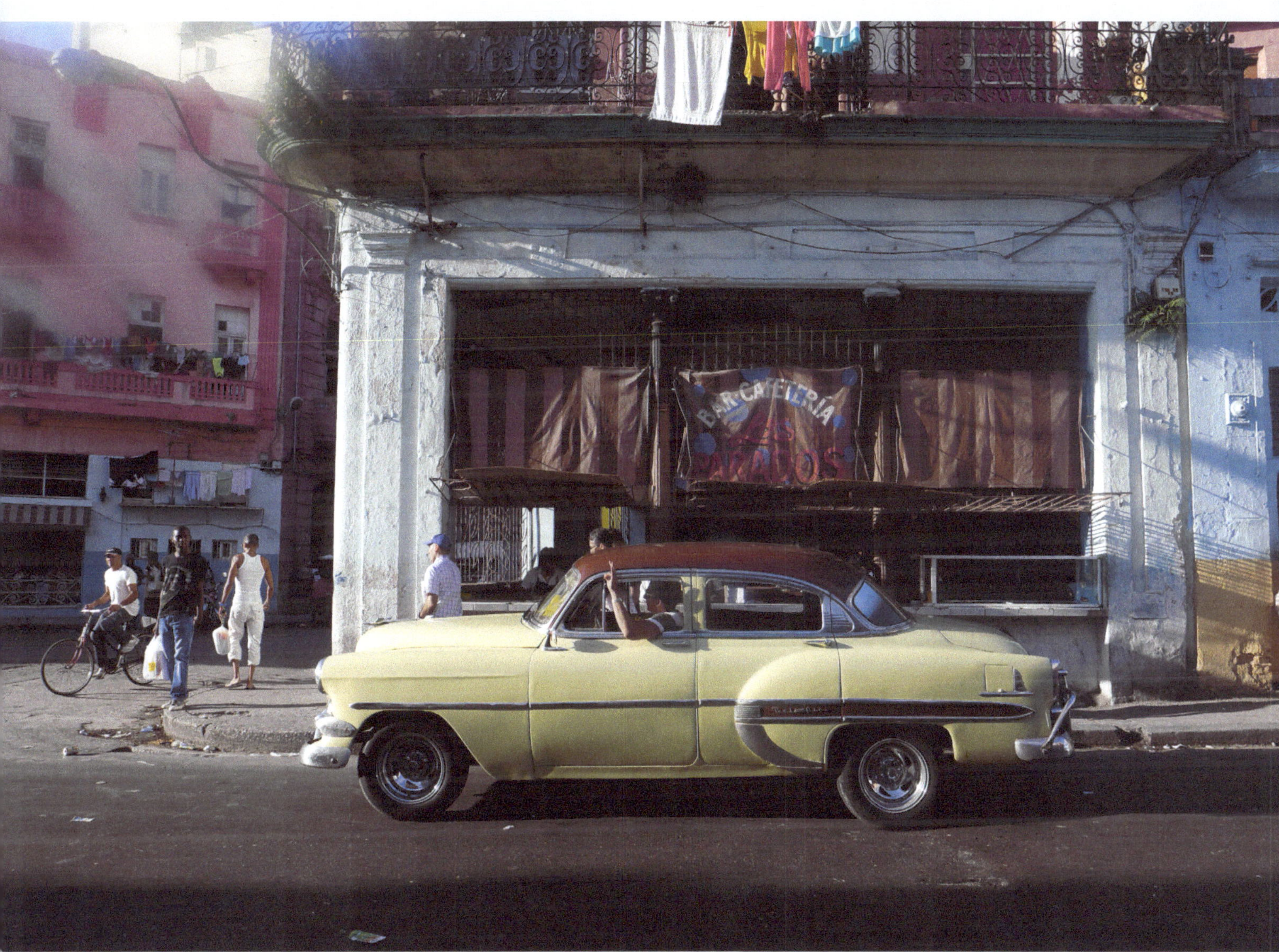

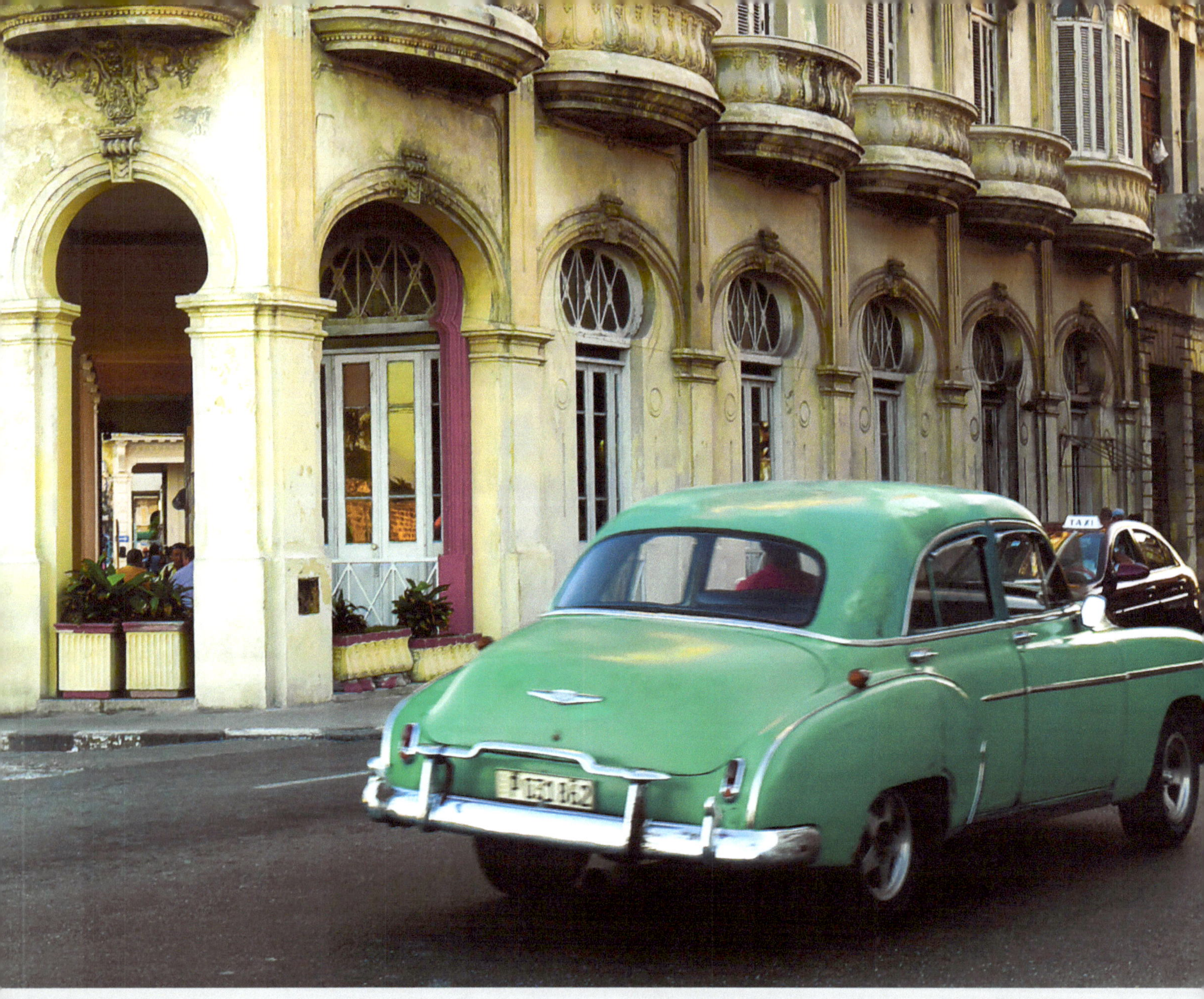

A contrast in color, Central Havana

Men resting in the shade on Calle de los Oficios

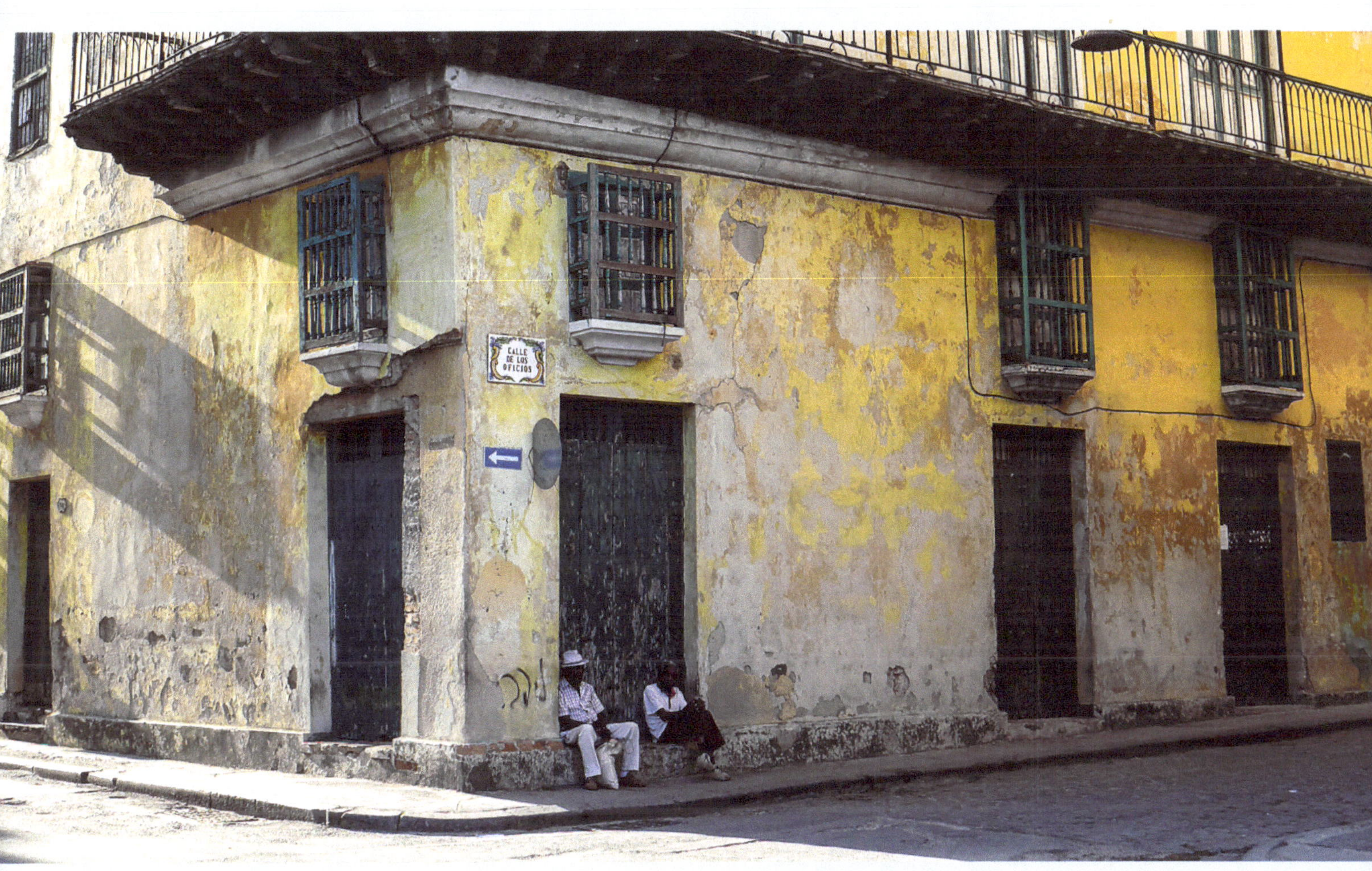

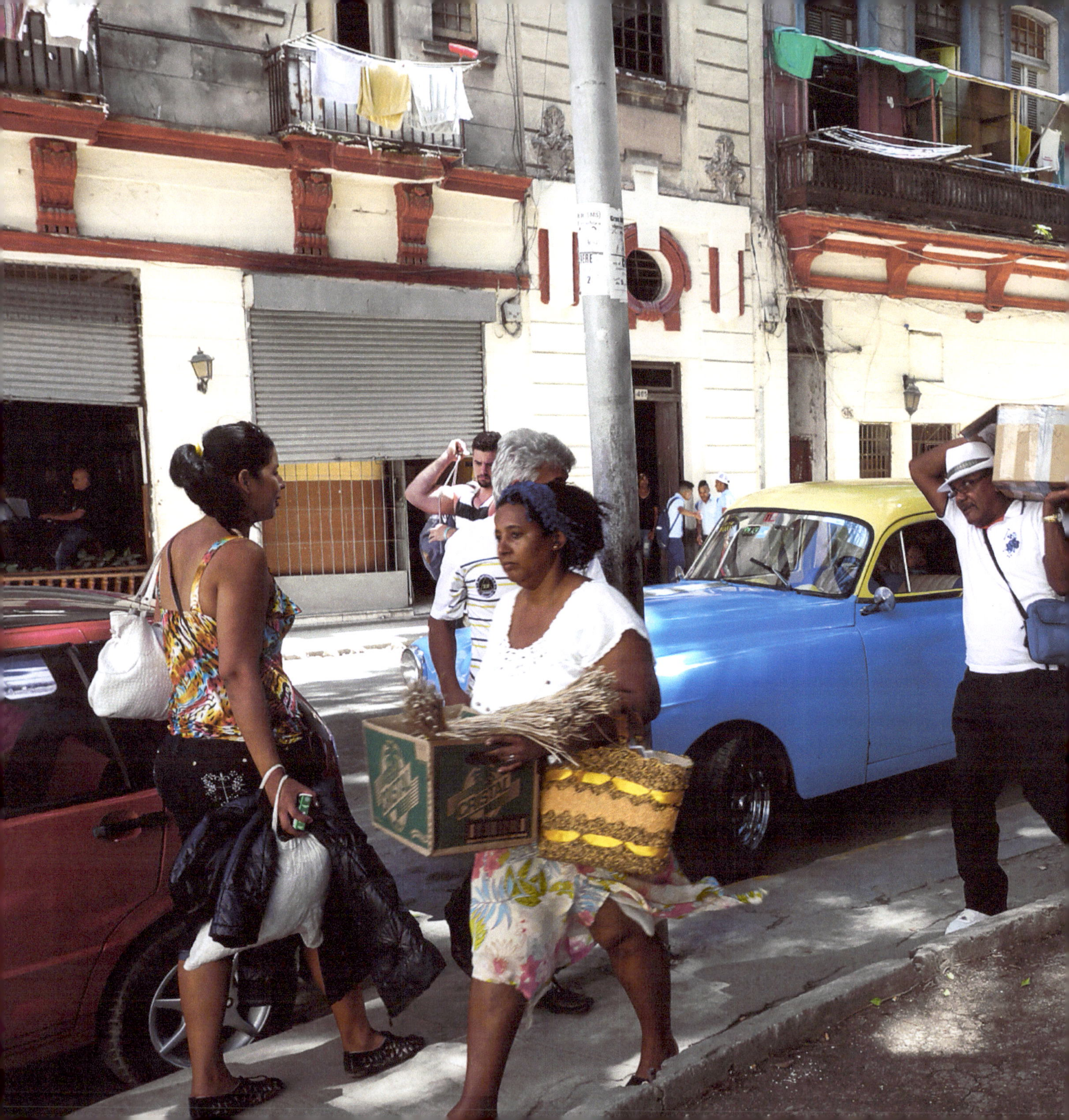

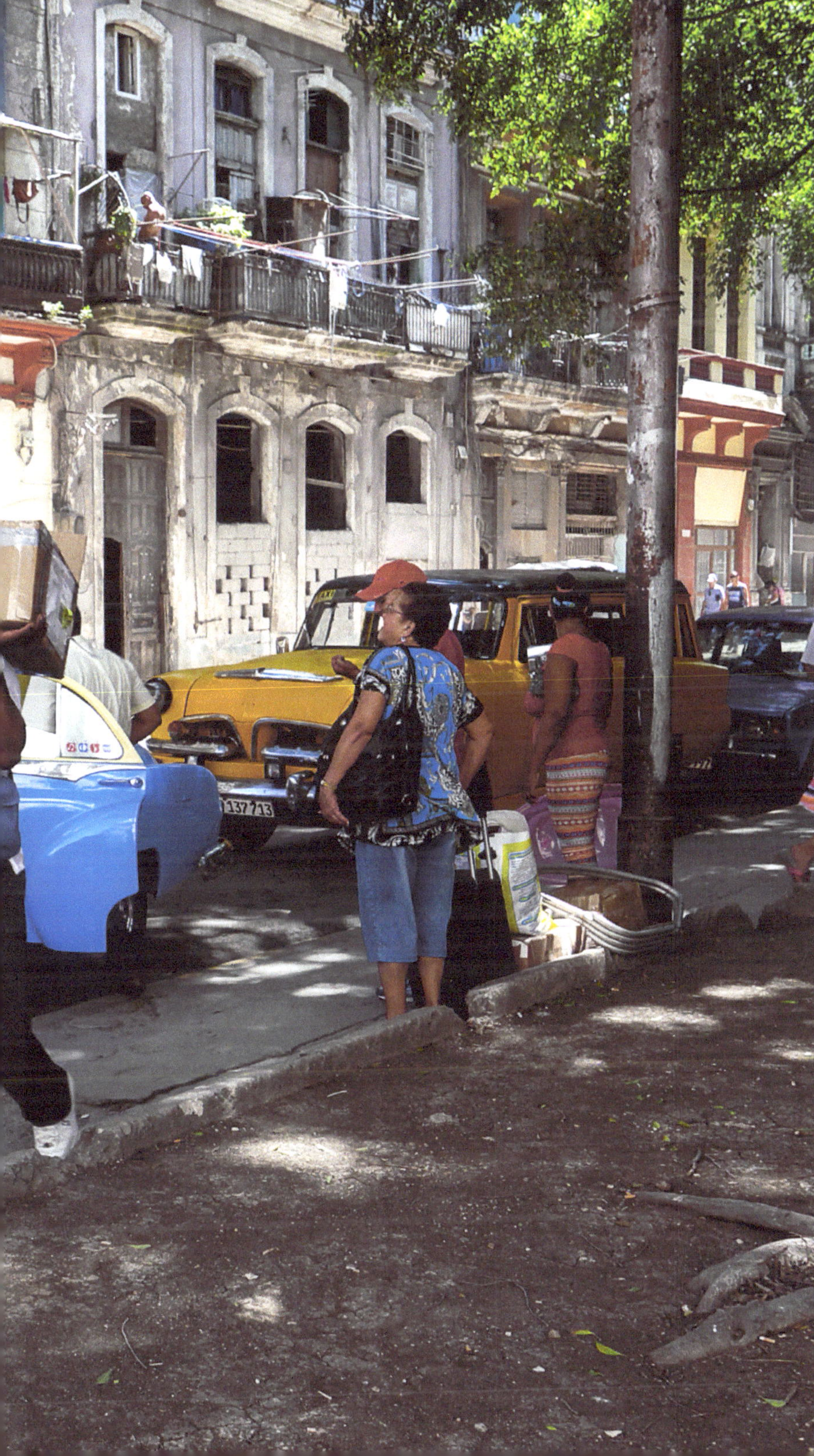

City scene of women running errands, Central Havana

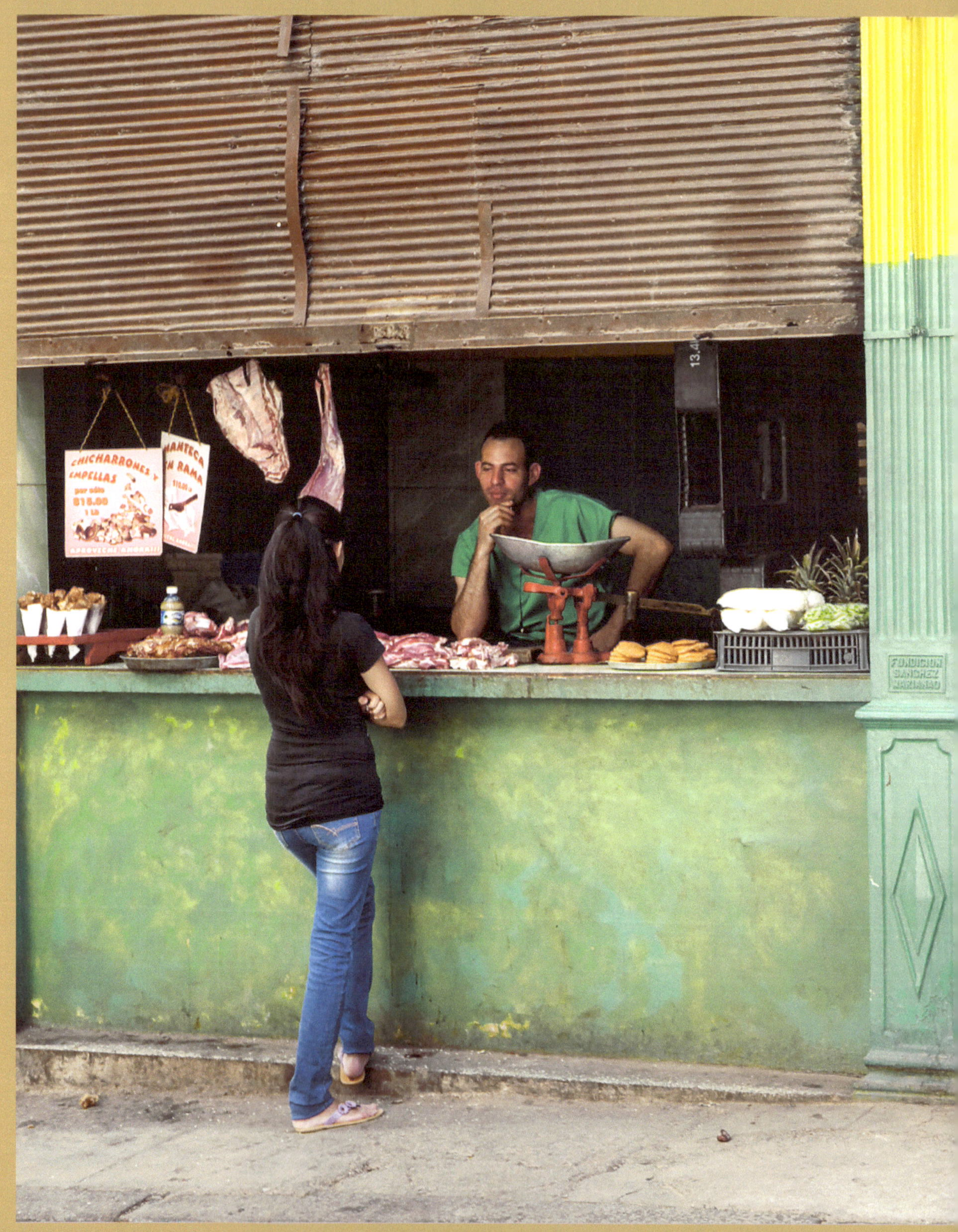
CHICHARRONES Y
EMPELLAS
APROVECHE AHORA!!!
FUNDICION
SANCHEZ

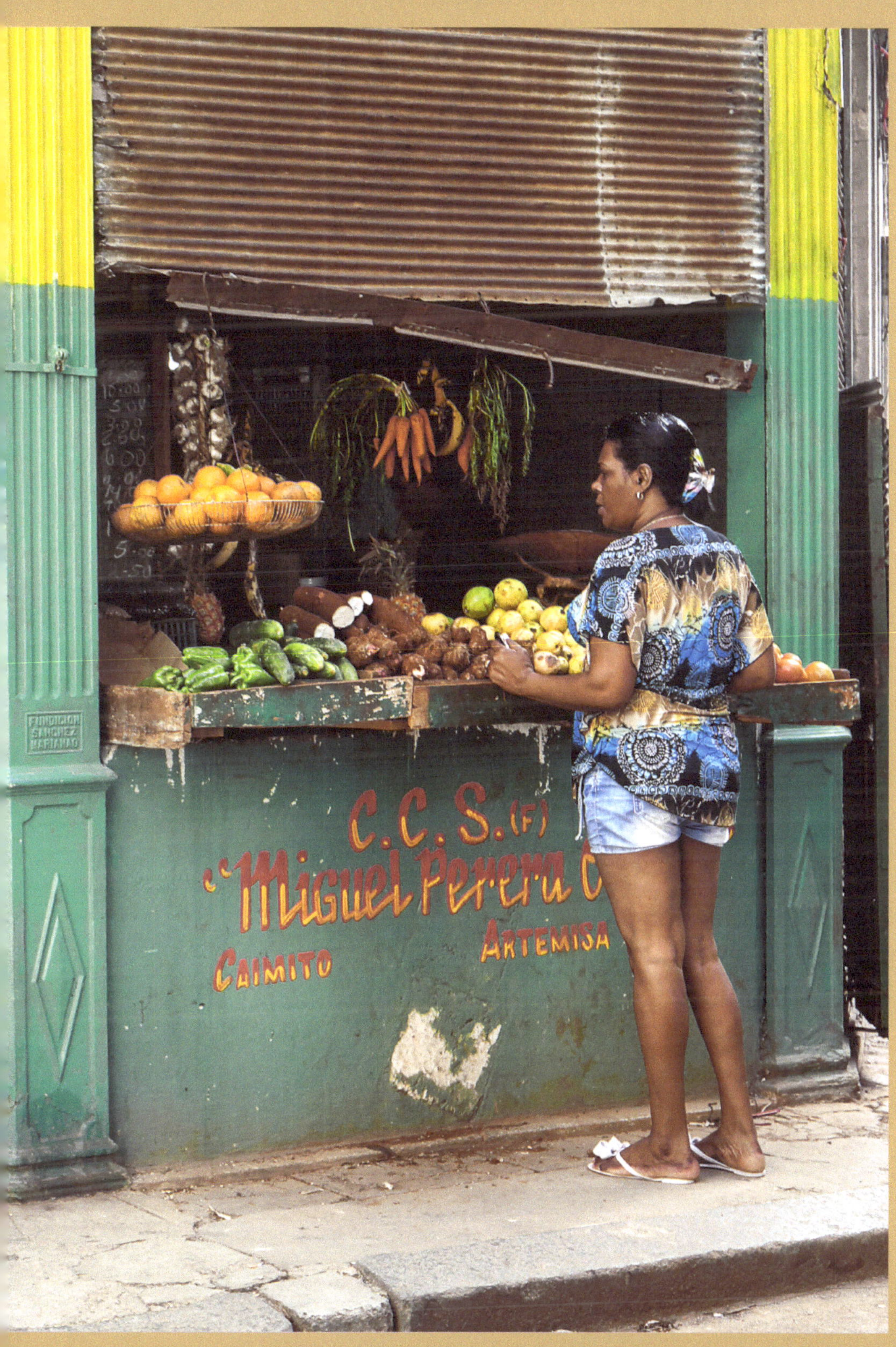

Butcher flirting with a patron; woman examining produce at a shop, Central Havana

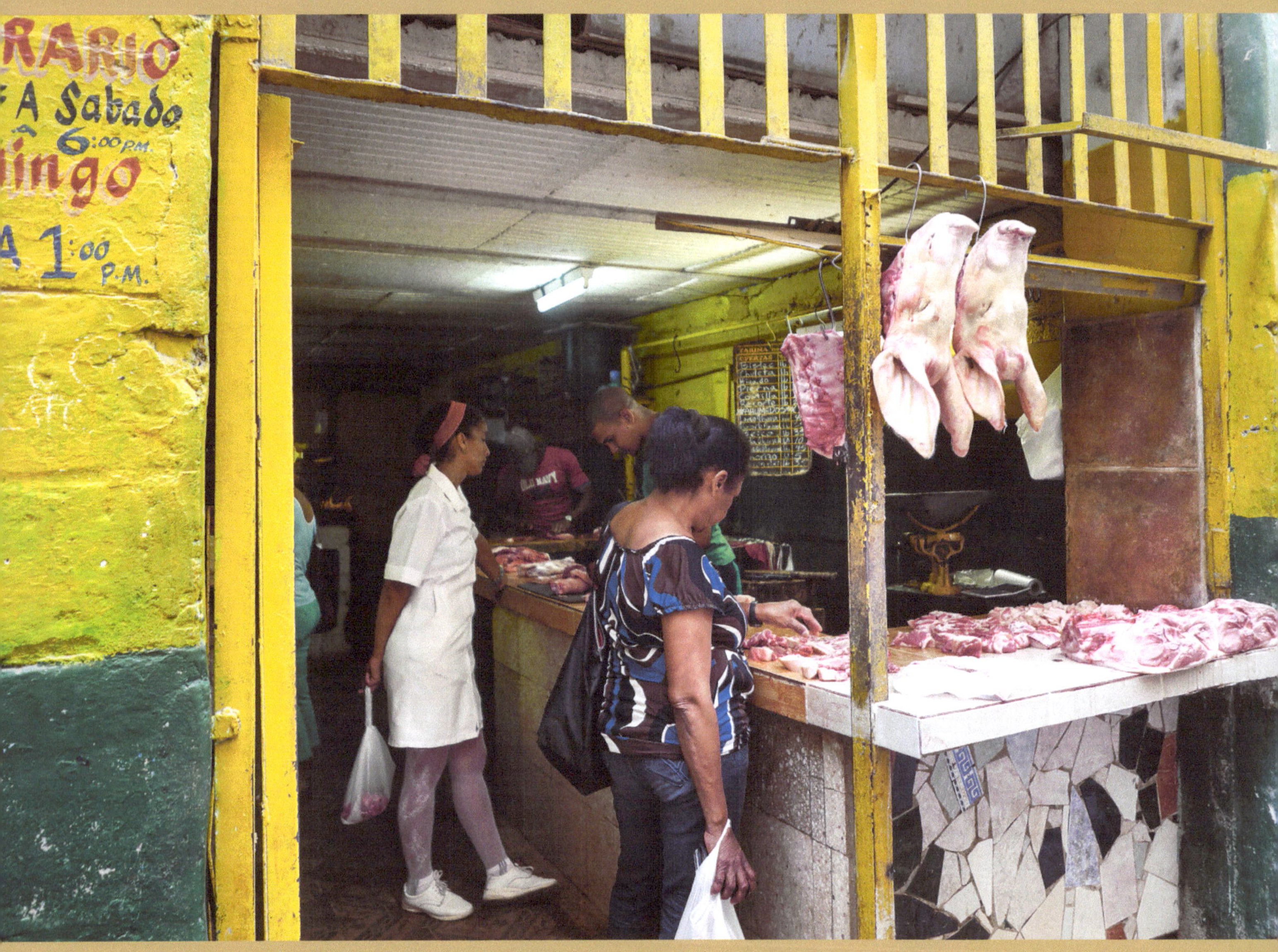

A butcher shop selling pork, Central Havana

The Hotel Nacional with moon in the sky

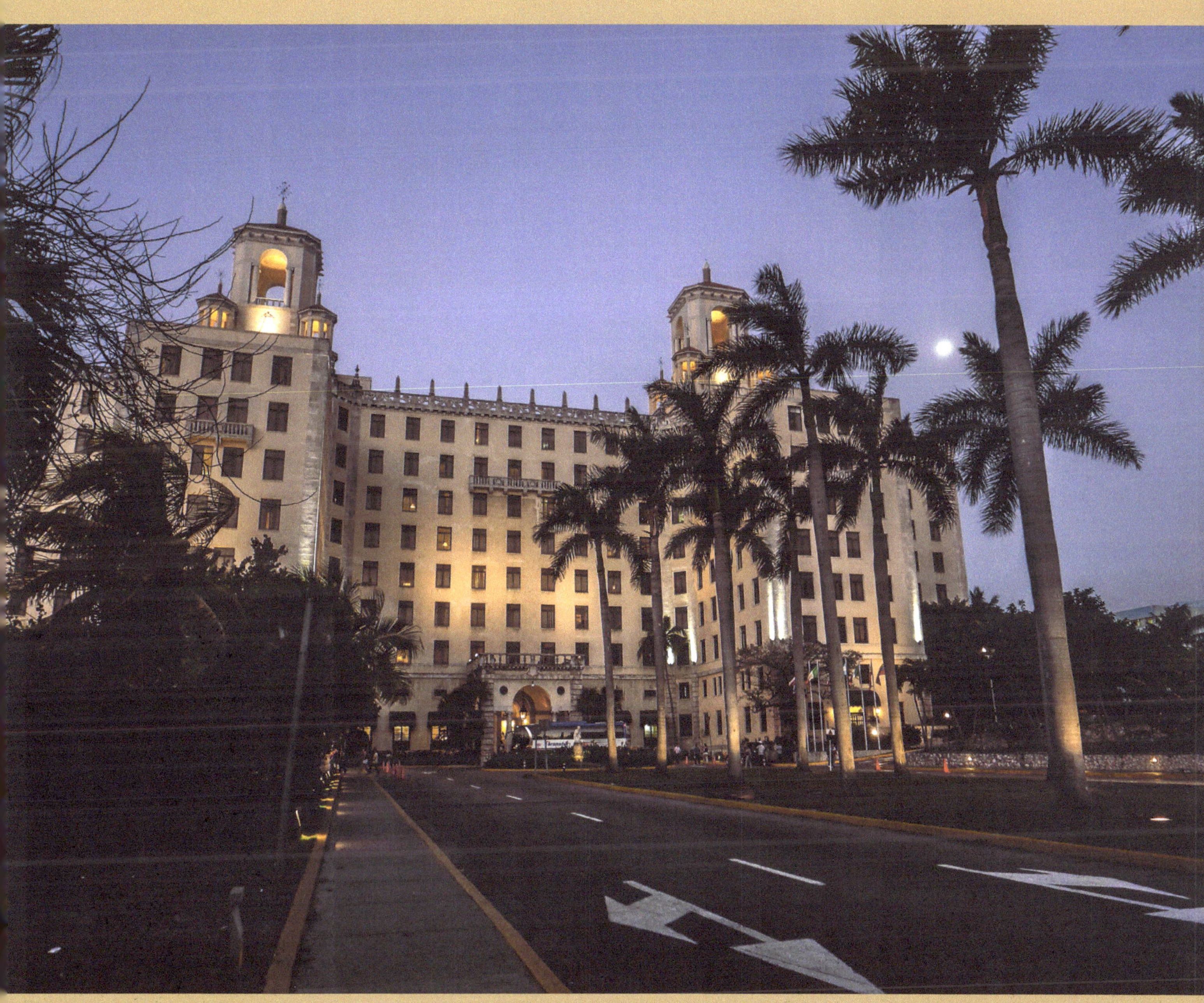

Man walking in Central Havana as the sun begins to set

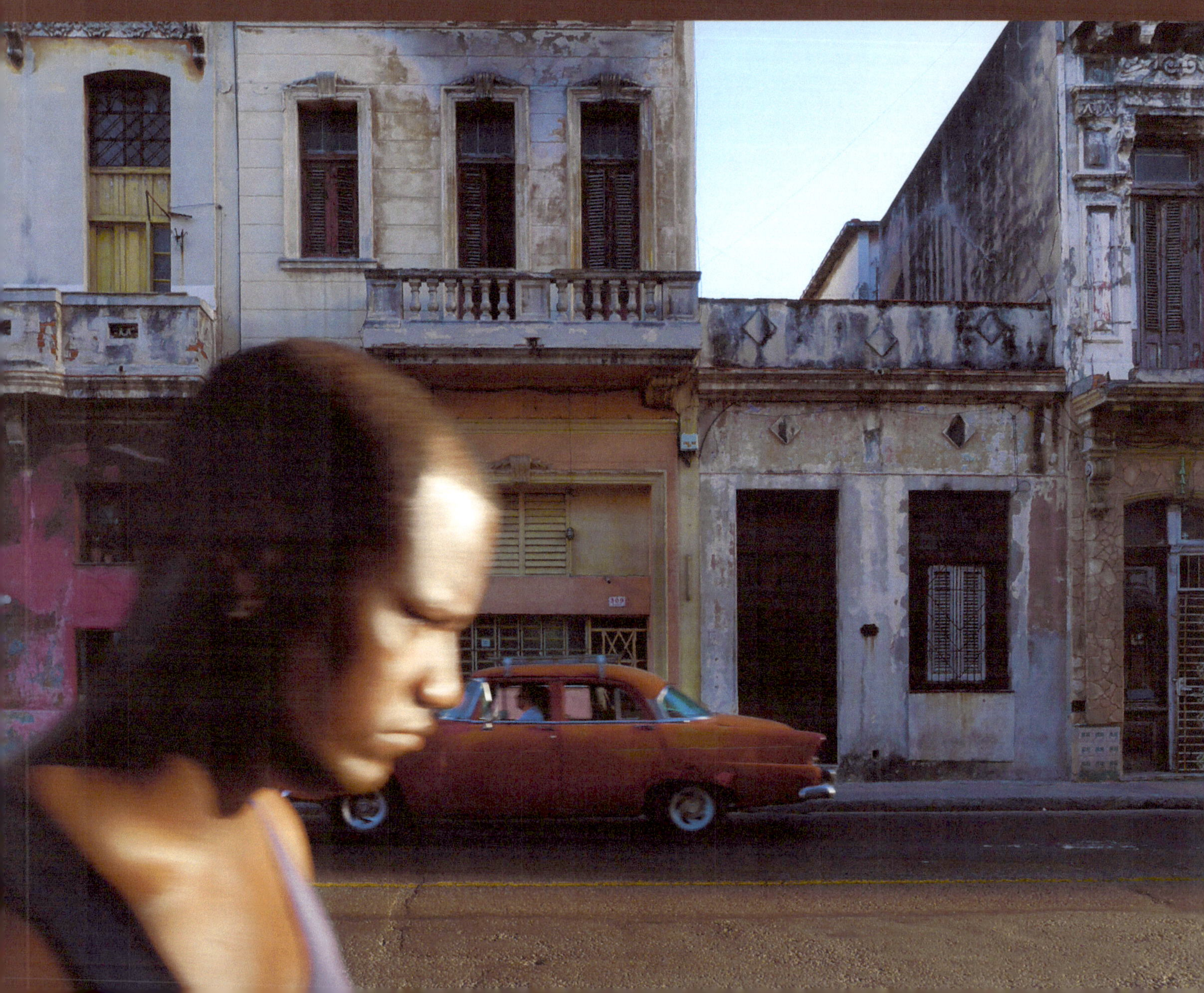

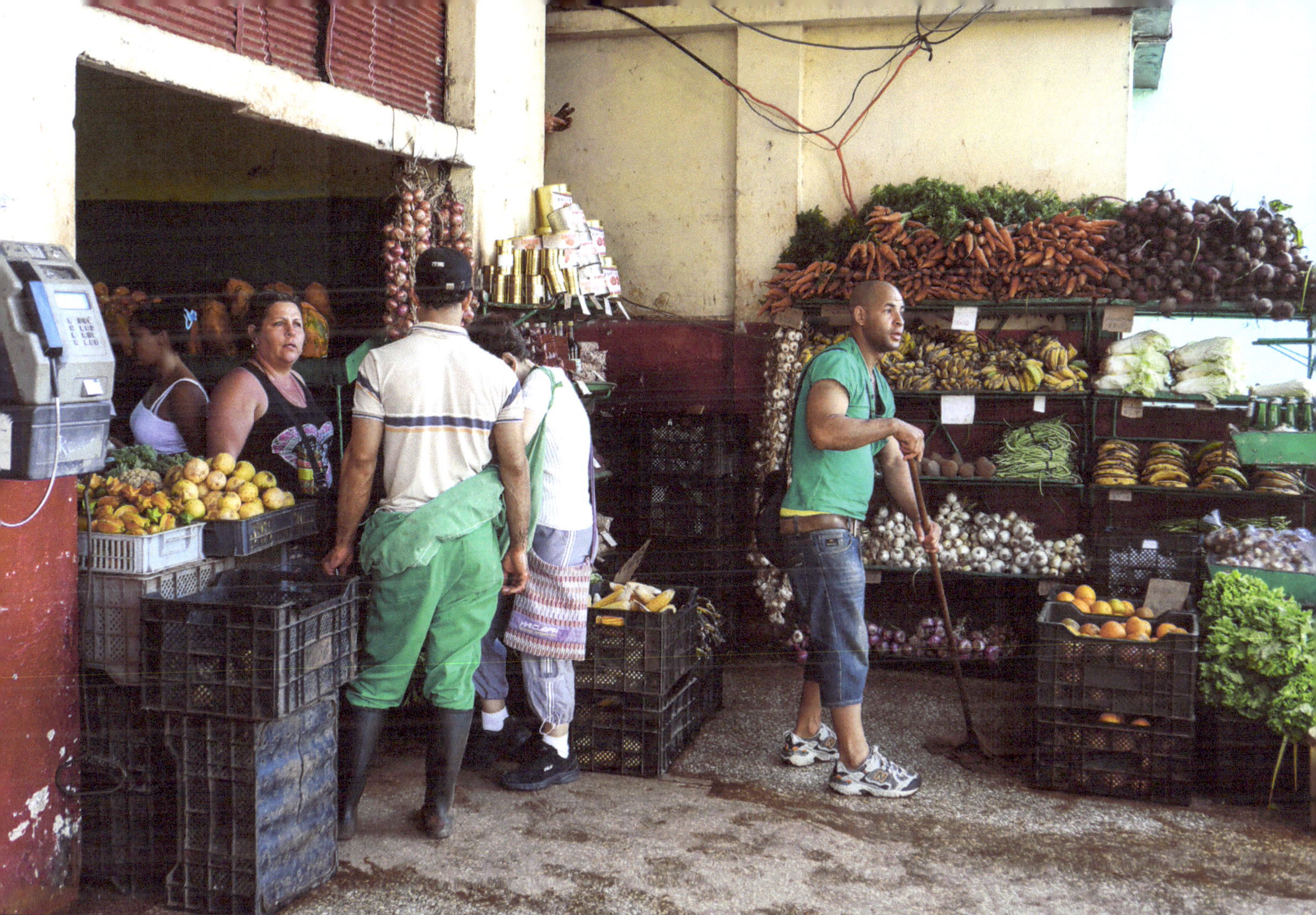

A free market fruit stand in Havana

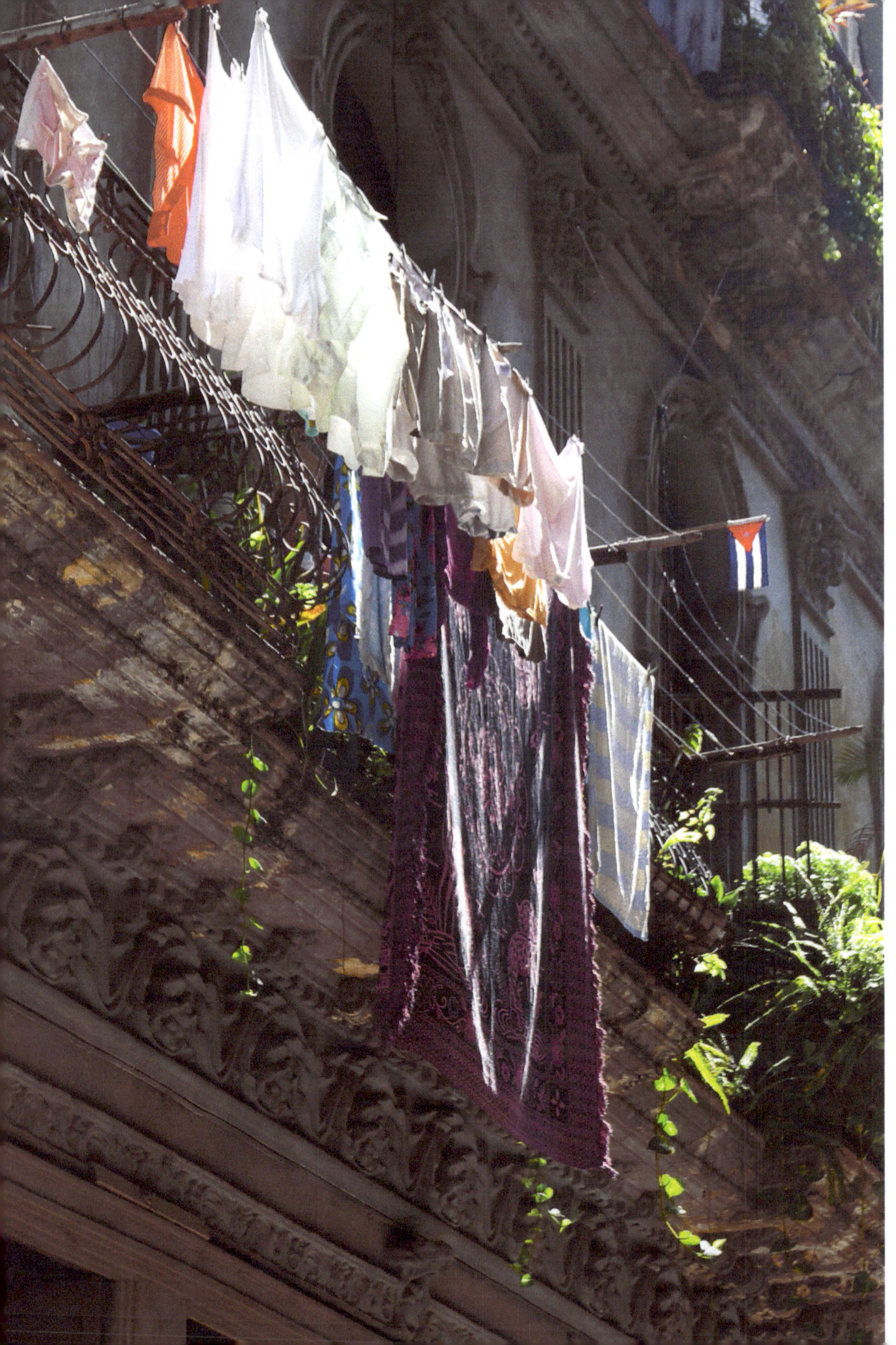

Laundry drying off a balcony in the Vedado; a Cuban flag

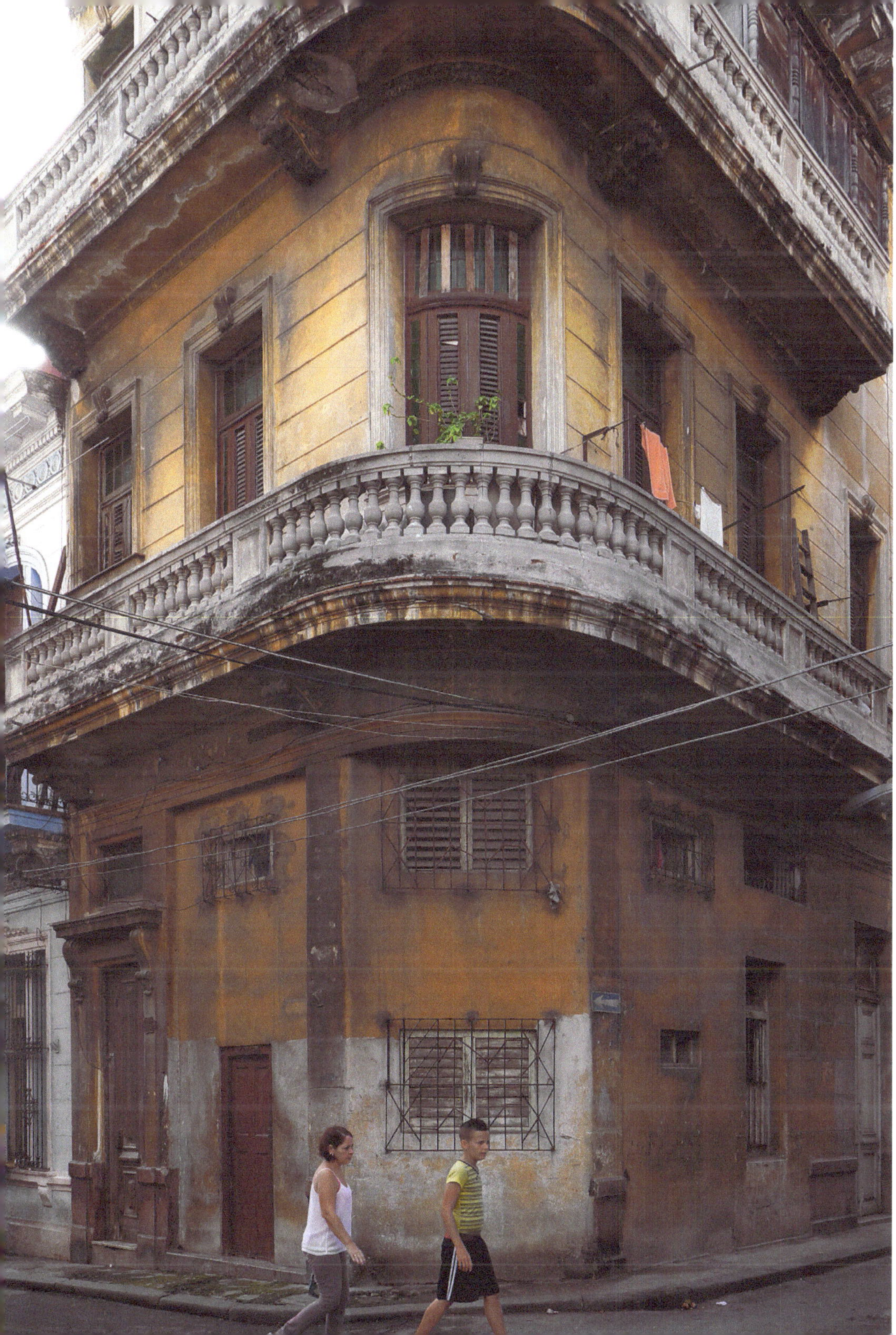

Mother and son walking in their neighborhood, Central Havana

A young couple spending time at dusk among other visitors to the seaside promenade at the Malecón

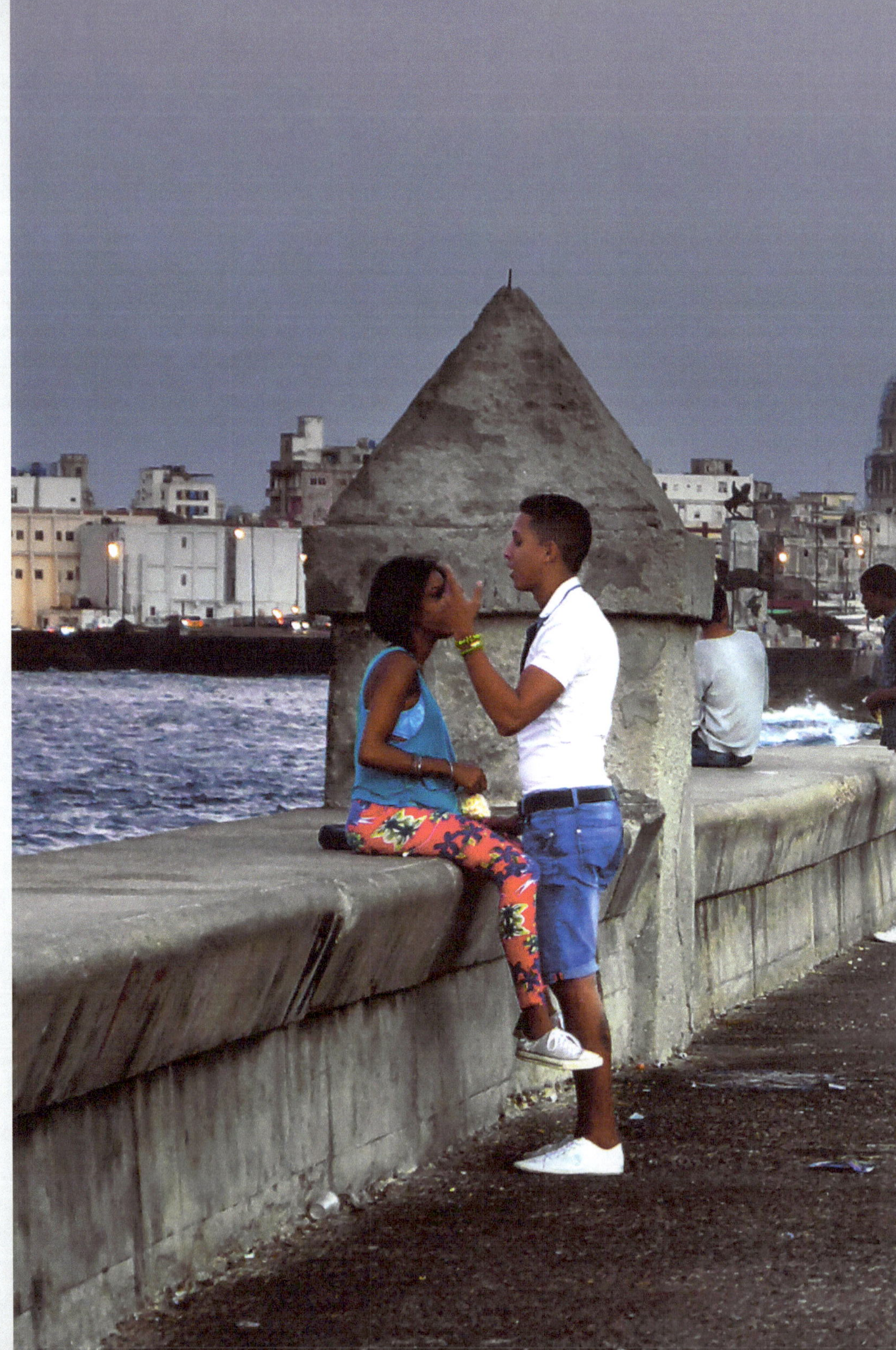

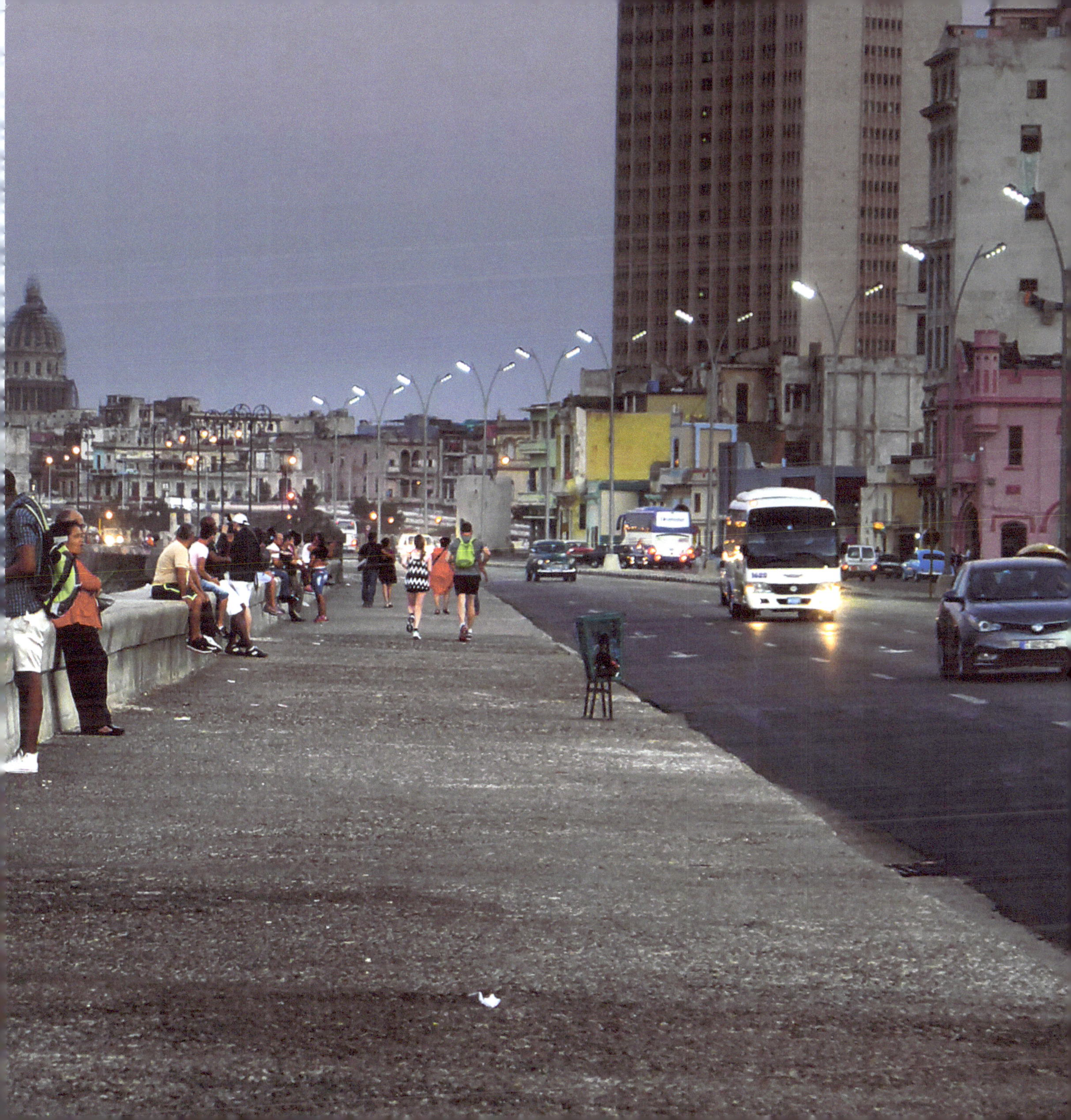

Books for sale in Old Havana—with a familiar theme

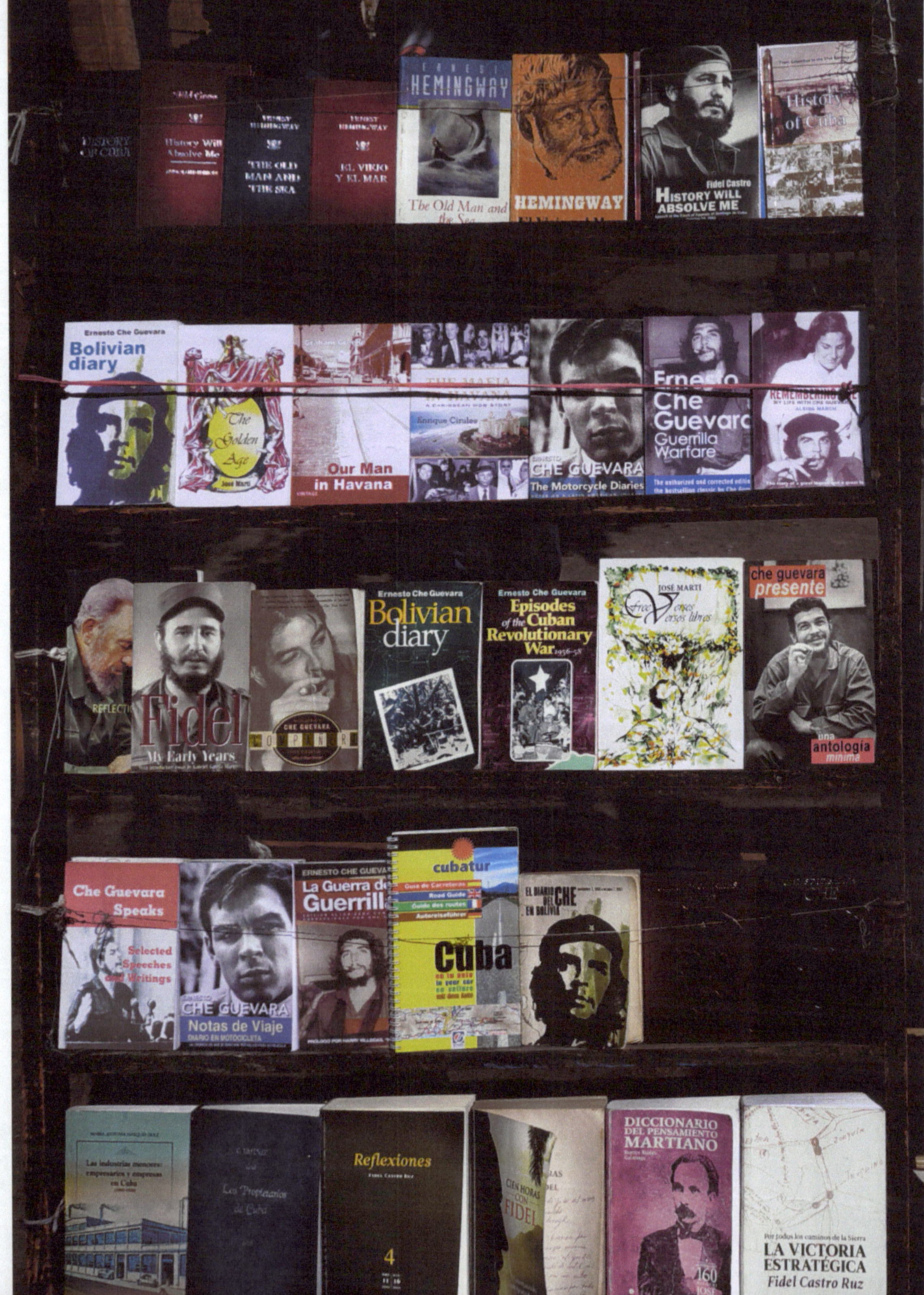

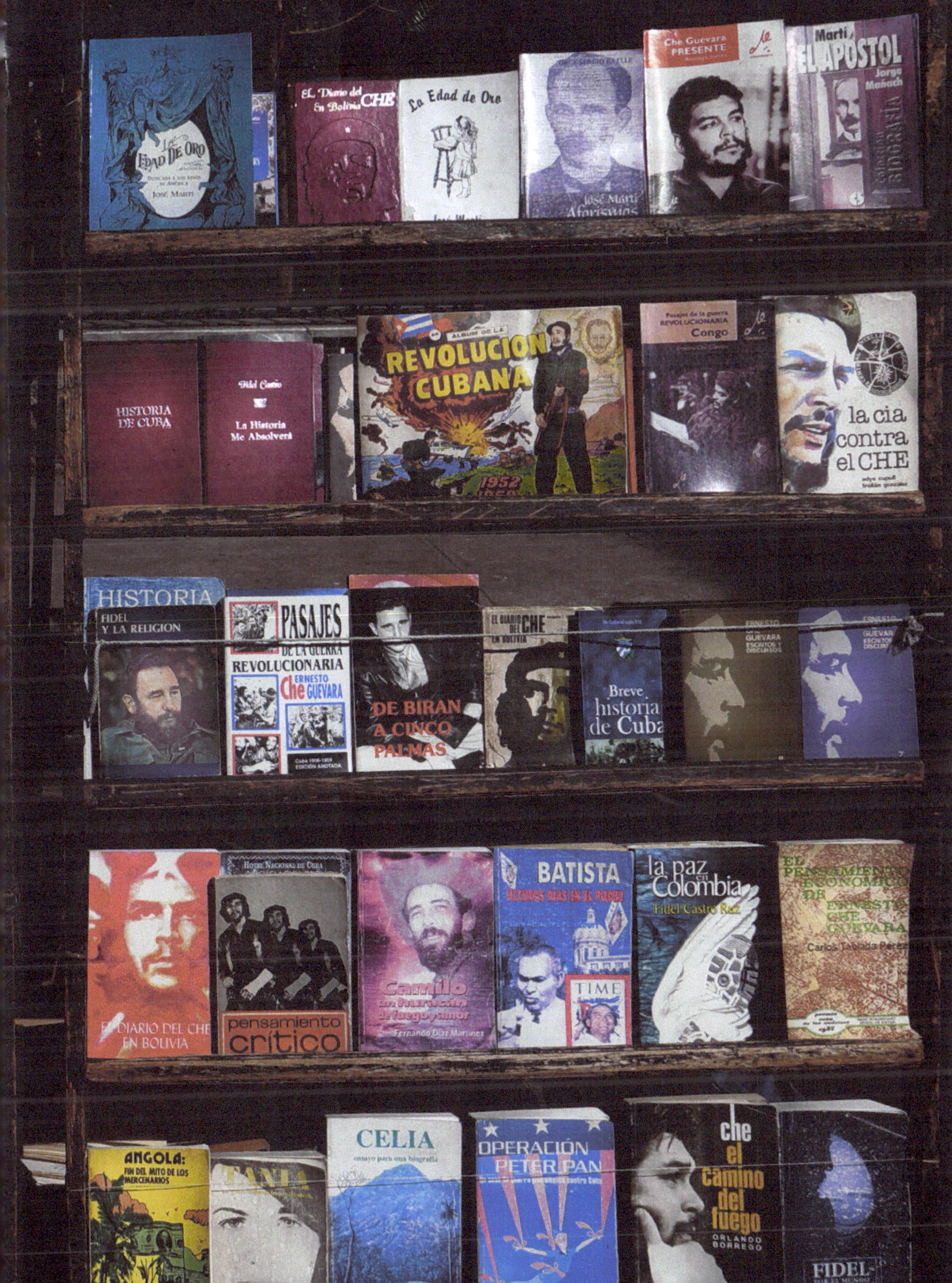
La Edad de Oro
José Martí
El Diario del CHE en Bolivia
La Edad de Oro
José Martí
Aforismos
Che Guevara
PRESENTE
Martí
EL APOSTOL
Jorge Mañach
Colección Biografía
HISTORIA DE CUBA
Fidel Castro
La Historia Me Absolverá
ALBUM DE LA
REVOLUCION CUBANA
1952
Pasajes de la guerra REVOLUCIONARIA
Congo
la cia contra el CHE
HISTORIA
FIDEL Y LA RELIGION
PASAJES DE LA GUERRA REVOLUCIONARIA
ERNESTO Che GUEVARA
Cuba 1956-1959
EDICIÓN ANOTADA
DE BIRAN A CINCO PALMAS
EL DIARIO DEL CHE EN BOLIVIA
Breve historia de Cuba
ERNESTO GUEVARA
ESCRITOS Y DISCURSOS
EL DIARIO DEL CHE EN BOLIVIA
HOTEL NACIONAL DE CUBA
pensamiento crítico
Camilo
un huracán de fuego y amor
Fernando Díaz Martínez
BATISTA
TIME
la paz en Colombia
Fidel Castro Ruz
EL PENSAMIENTO ECONÓMICO DE ERNESTO CHE GUEVARA
Carlos Tablada Pérez
ANGOLA:
FIN DEL MITO DE LOS MERCENARIOS
TANIA
CELIA
ensayo para una biografía
OPERACIÓN PETER PAN
che el camino del fuego
ORLANDO BORREGO
FIDEL

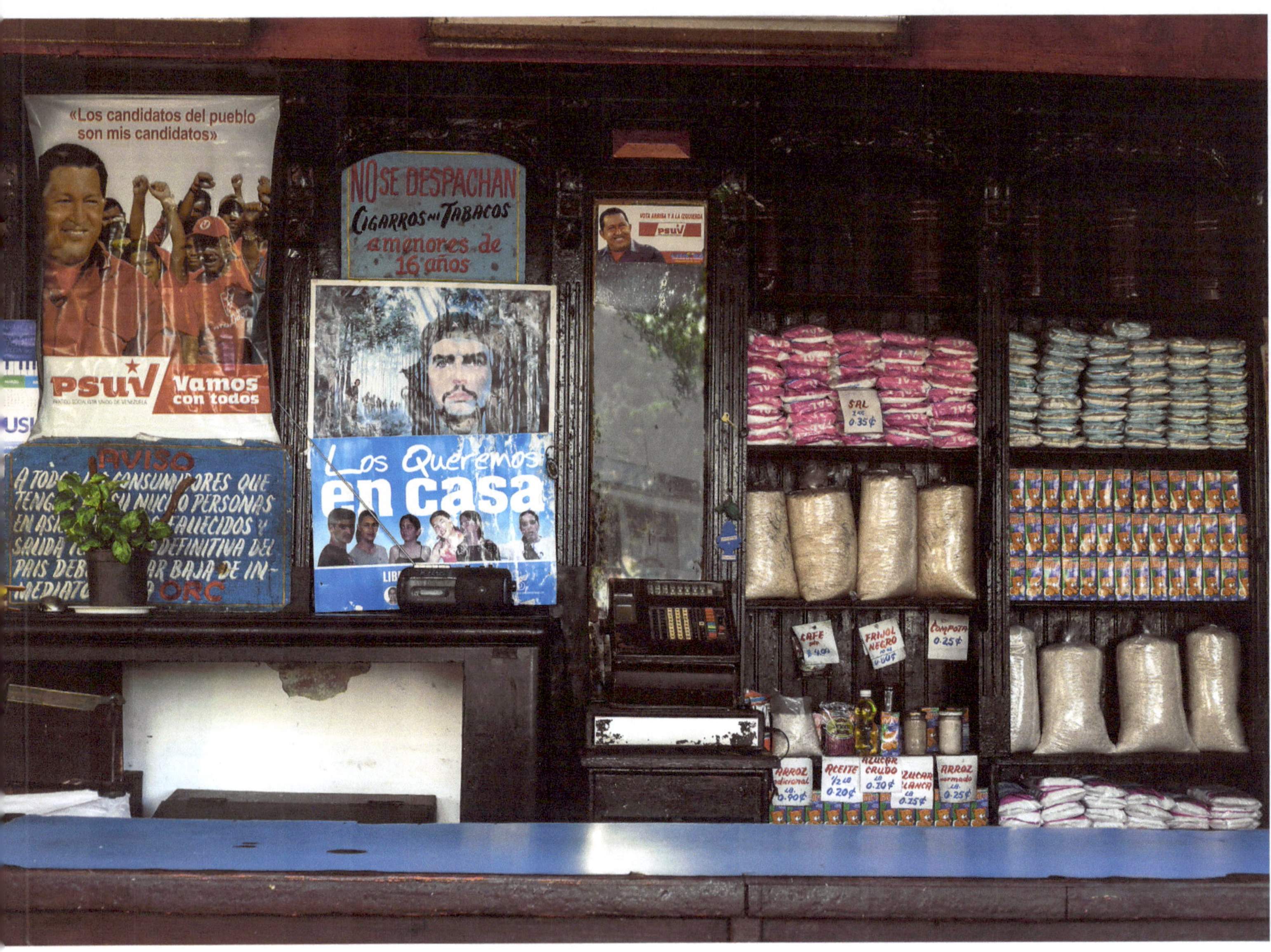

Salt, rice, sugar, coffee, and other products for sale among mementos of Ernesto "Che" Guevara and Hugo Chávez

A worker, taking care of the dead

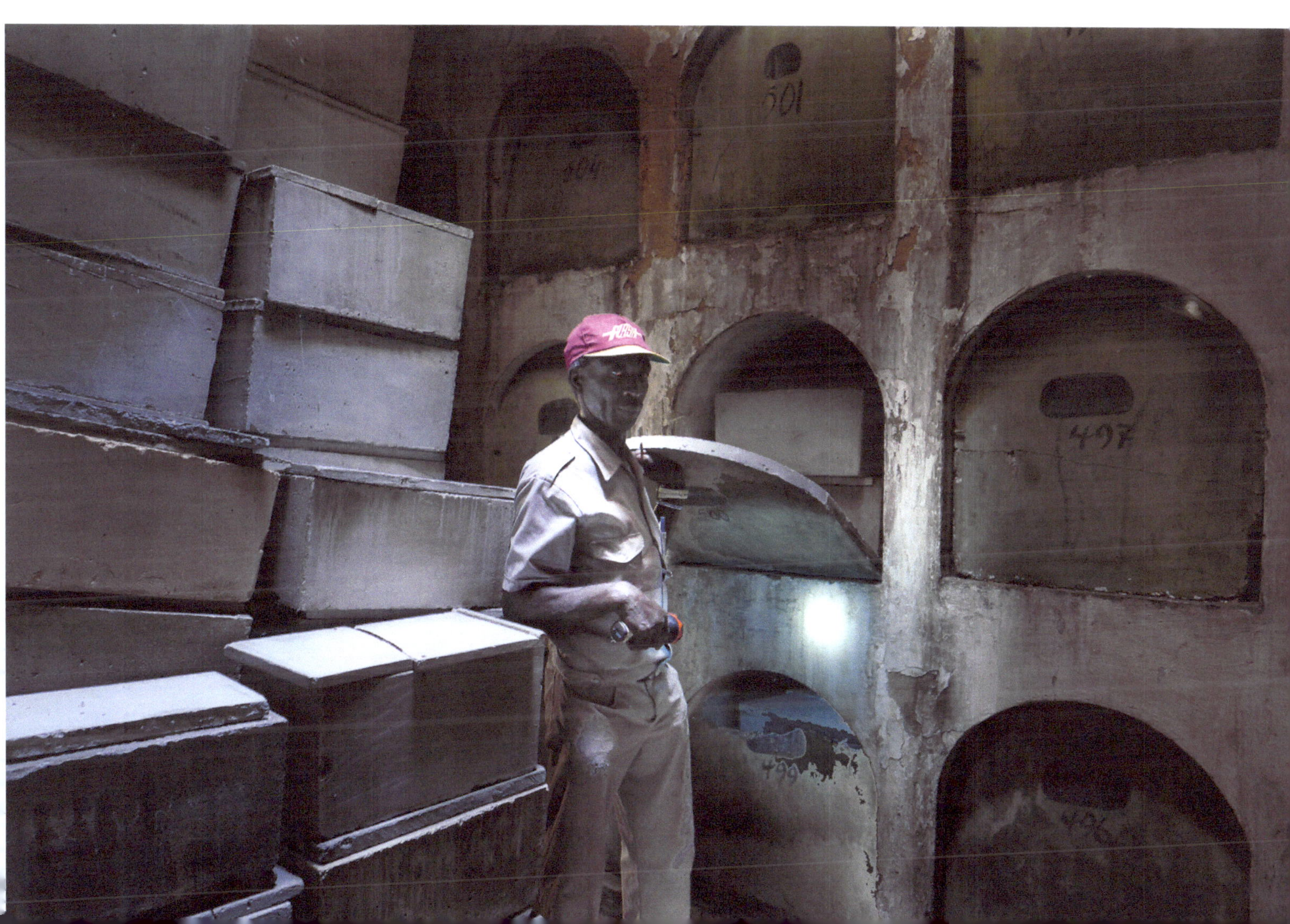

Trinidad

View of the Cuban landscape from a belfry

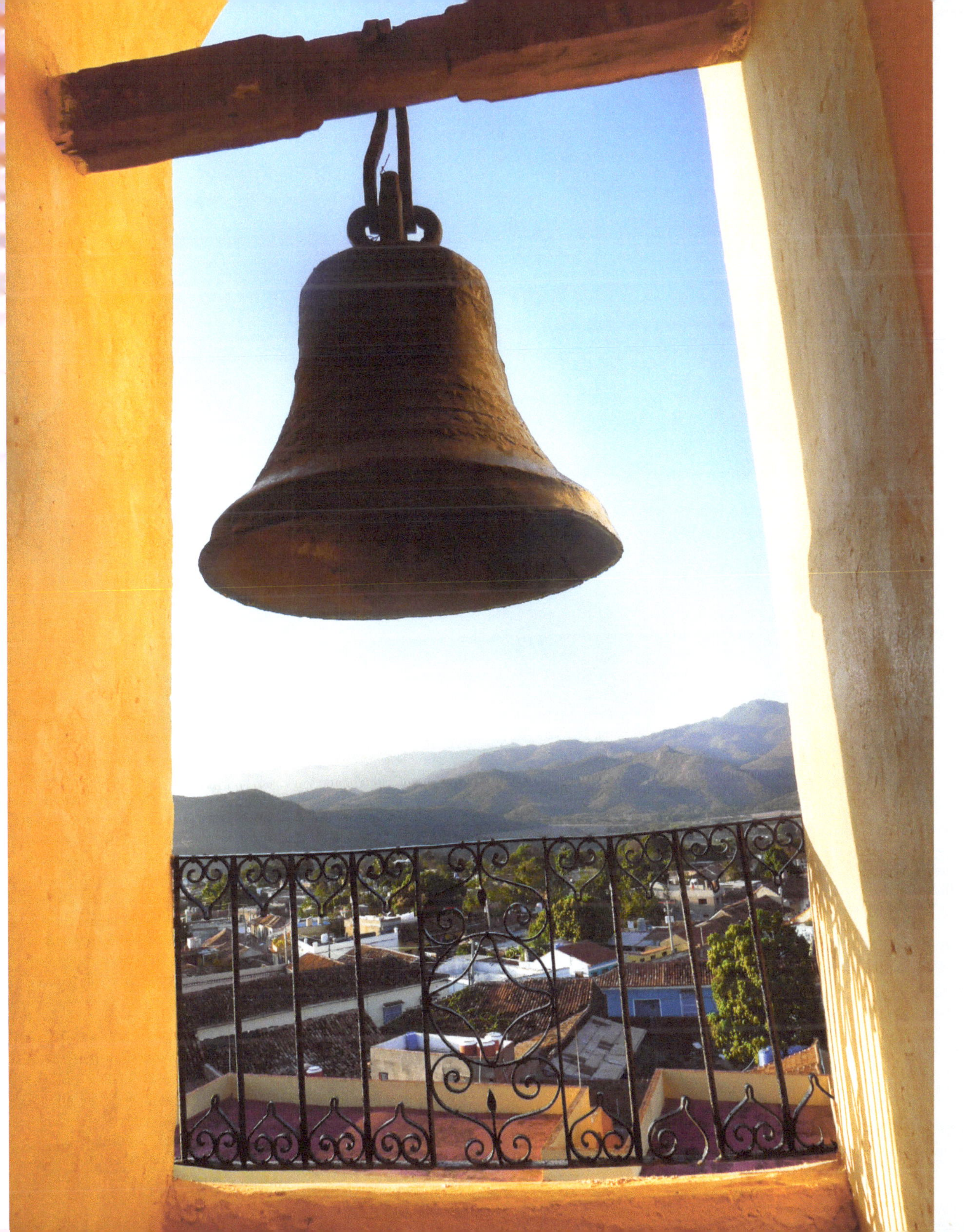

"Mountains culminate in peaks, and nations in men." José Martí

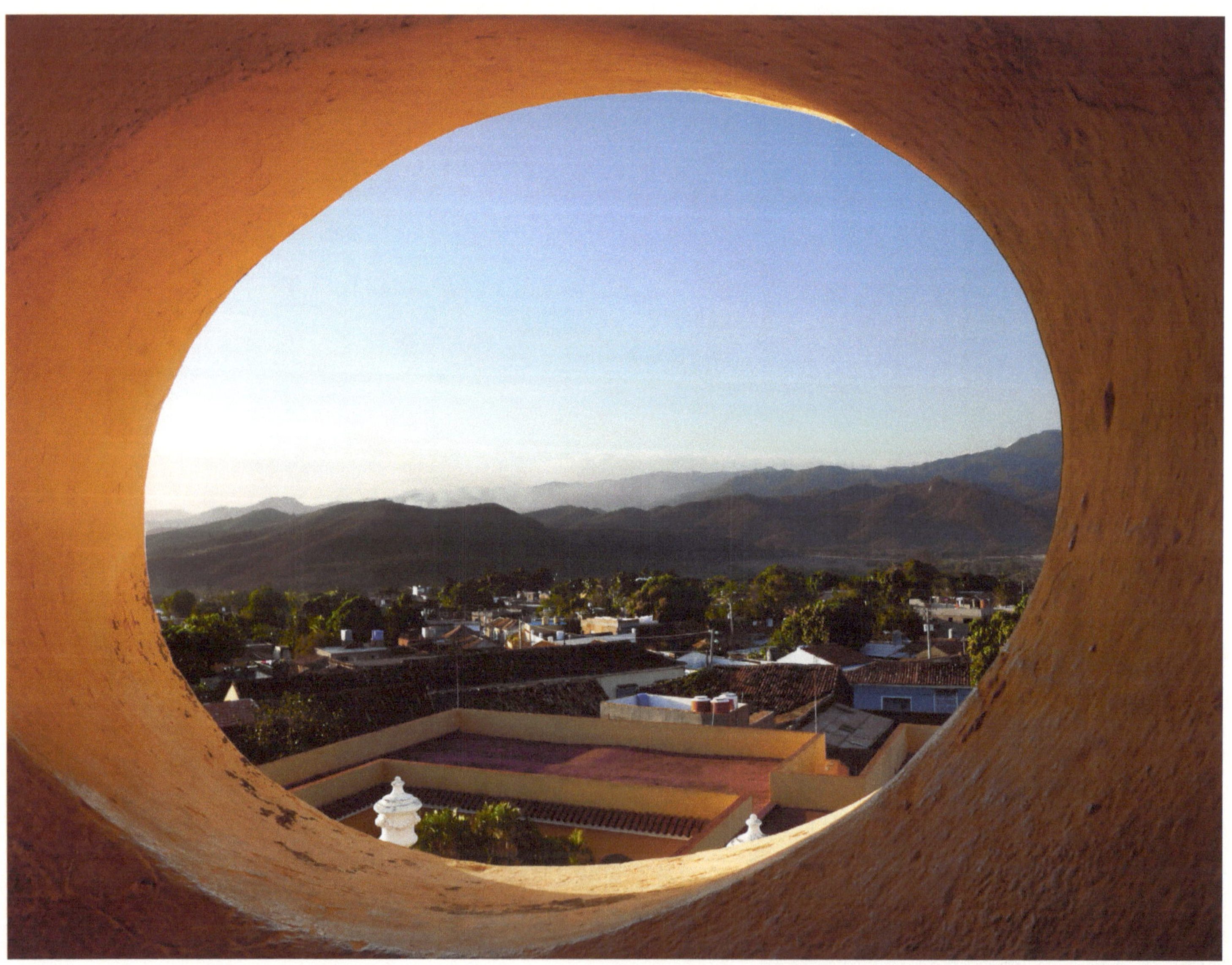

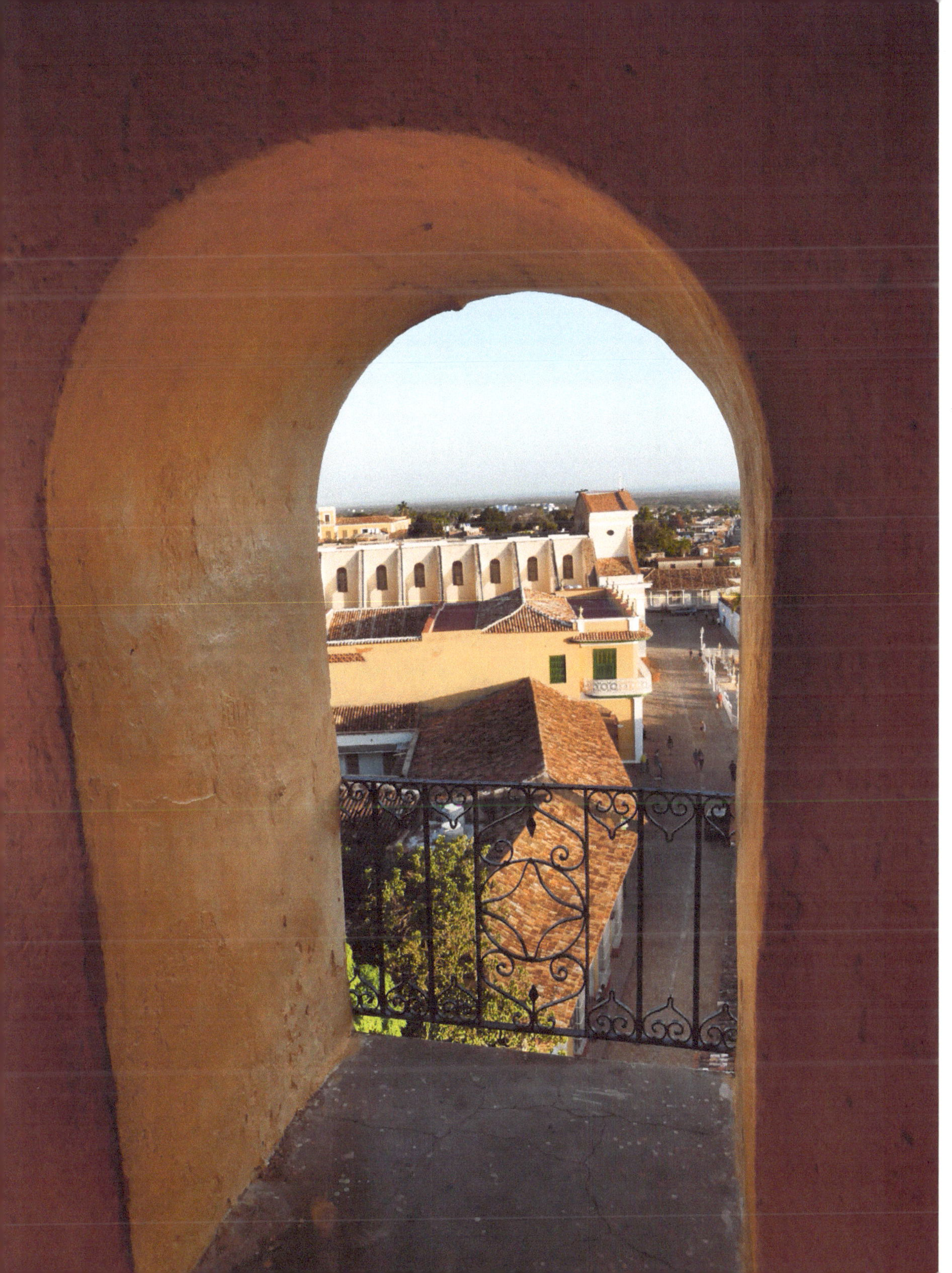

"Cuando salí de Cuba deje enterrado mi corazón,"
Celia Cruz

A man enjoying a cigar on a quiet afternoon

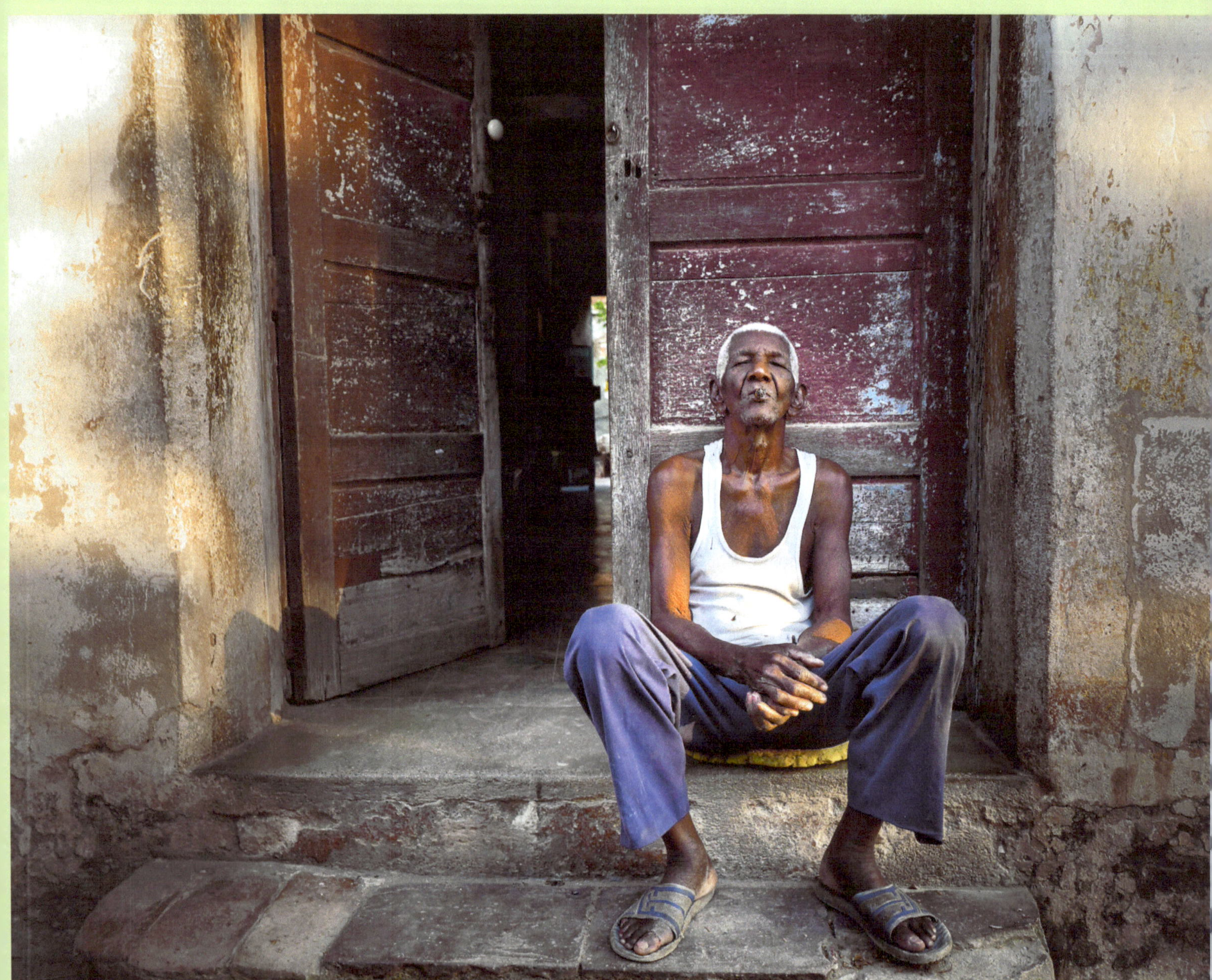

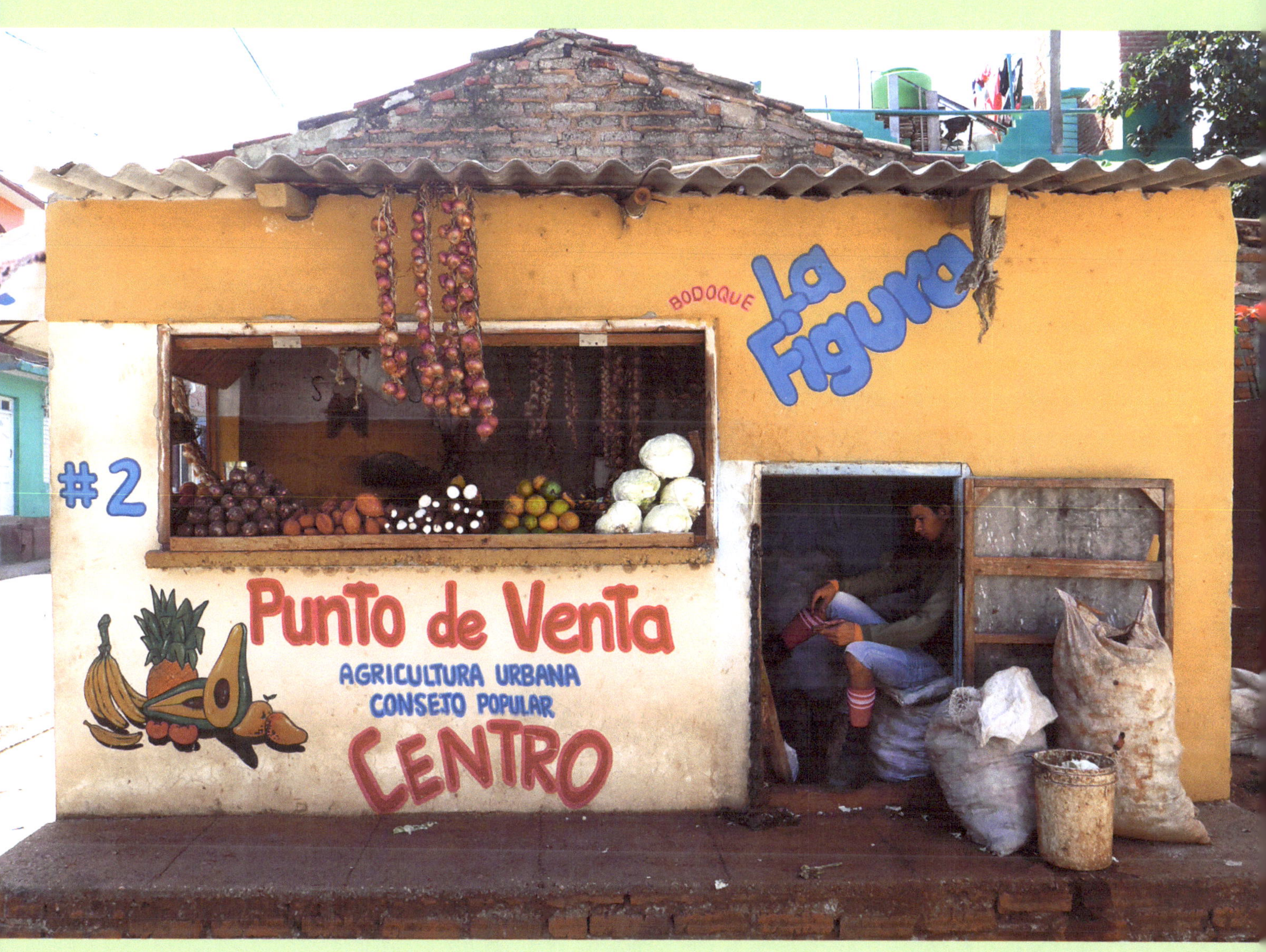

A fruit and vegetable market

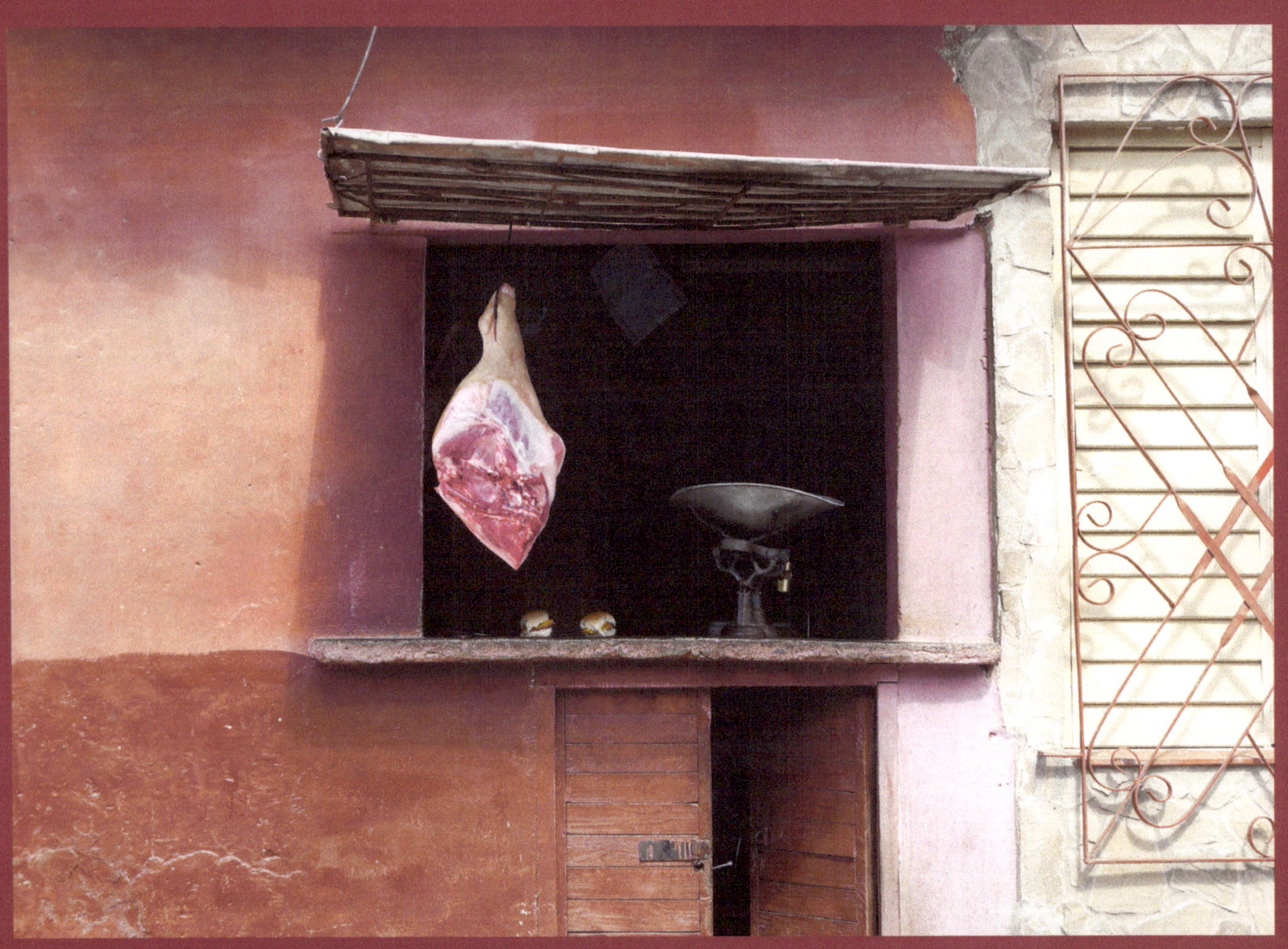

Two sandwiches resting on the counter of a butcher shop

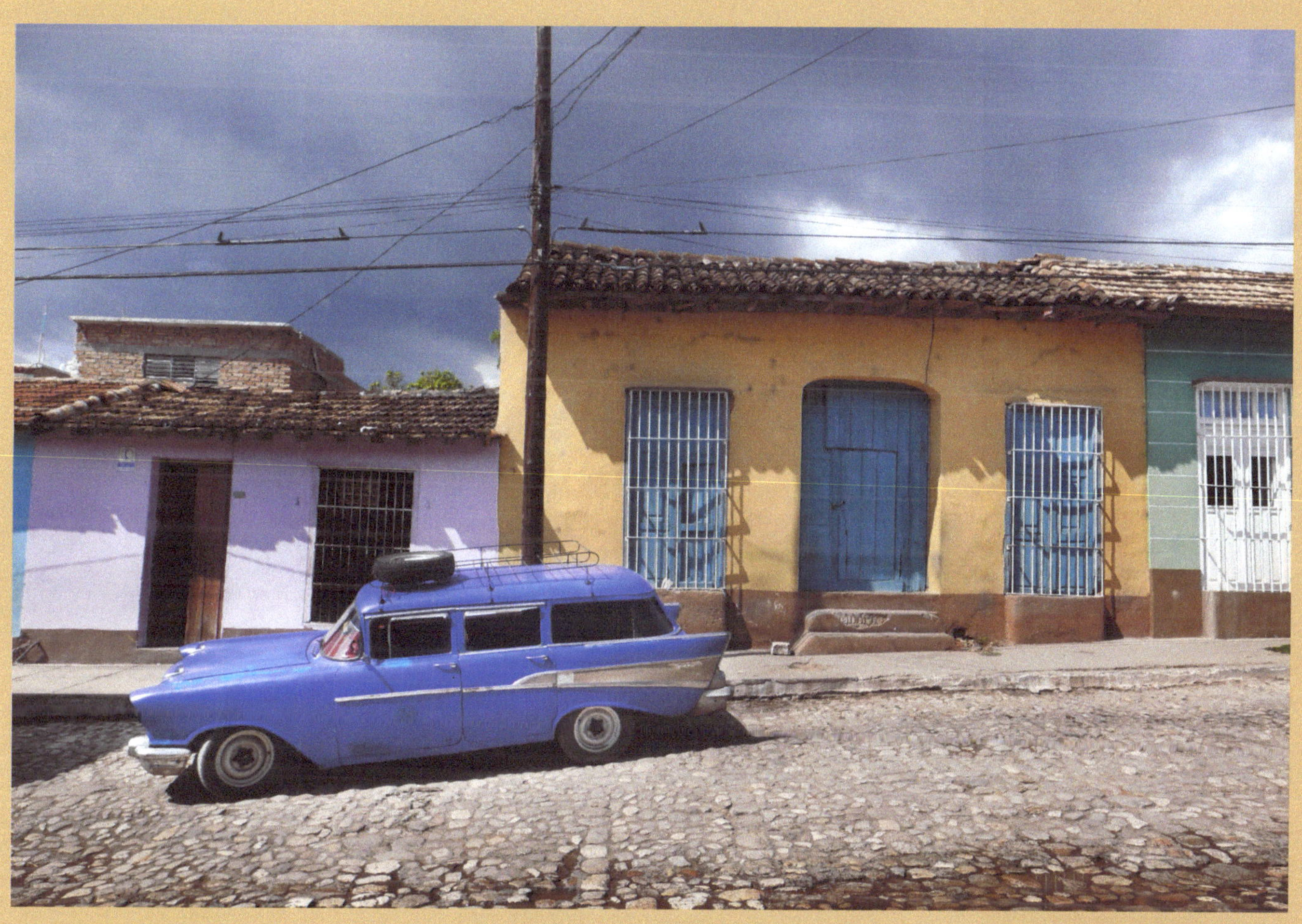

"Charm is a product of the unexpected," José Martí

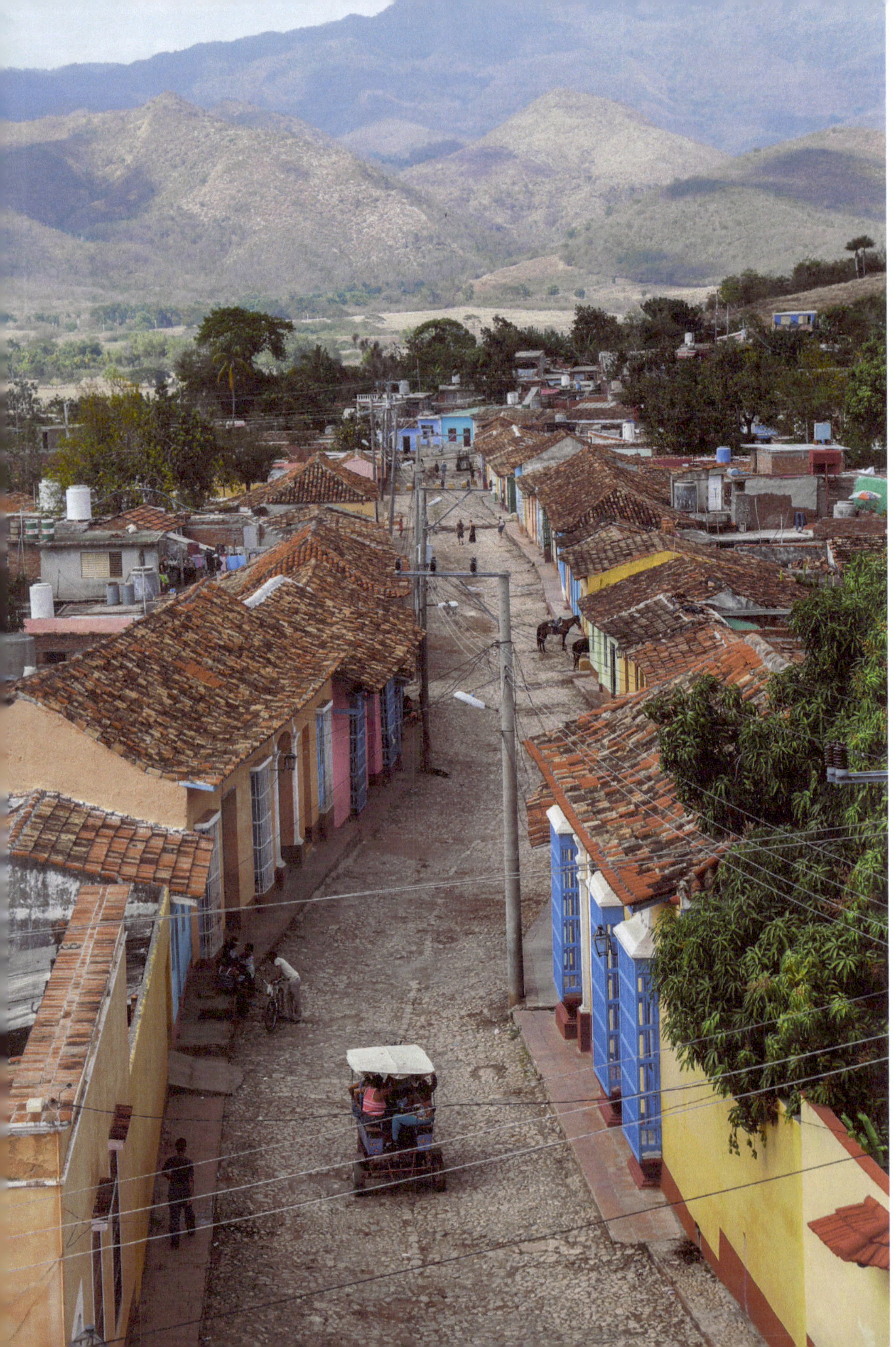

"Capitalism has neither the capacity, nor the morality, nor the ethics to solve the problems of poverty," Fidel Castro

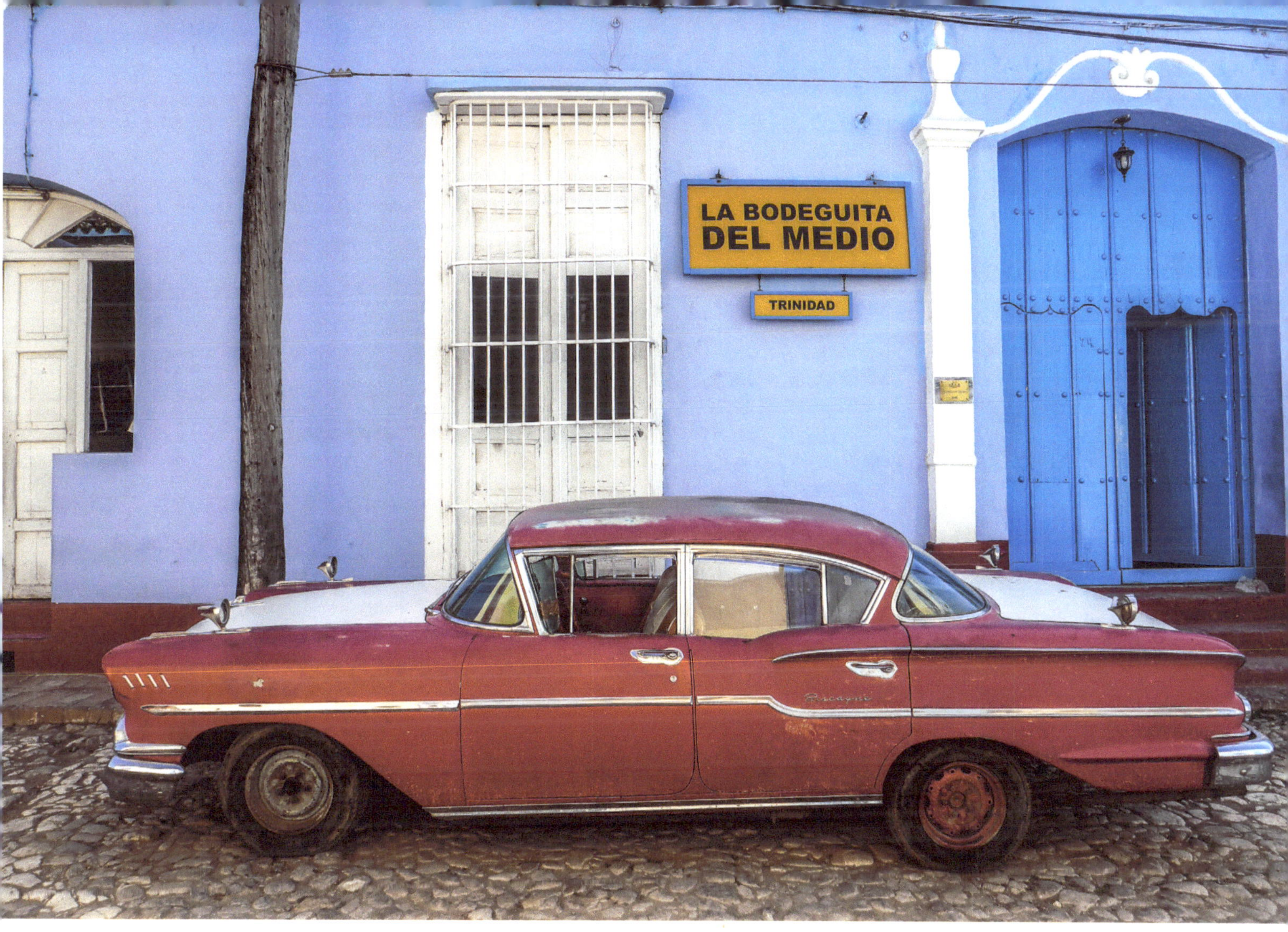

Stylish vintage American car in front of La Bodeguita del Medio bar

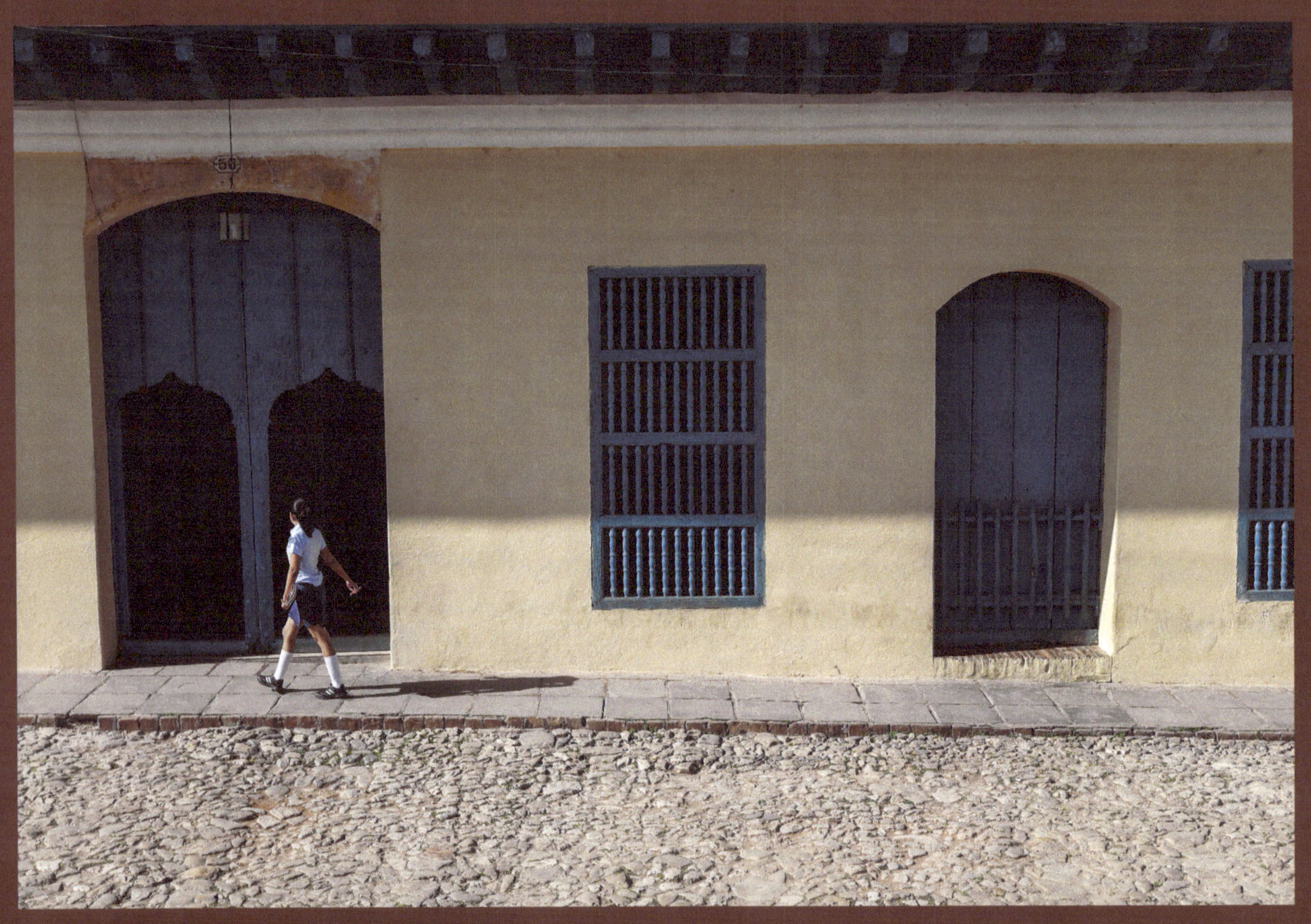

A schoolgirl on her way to class

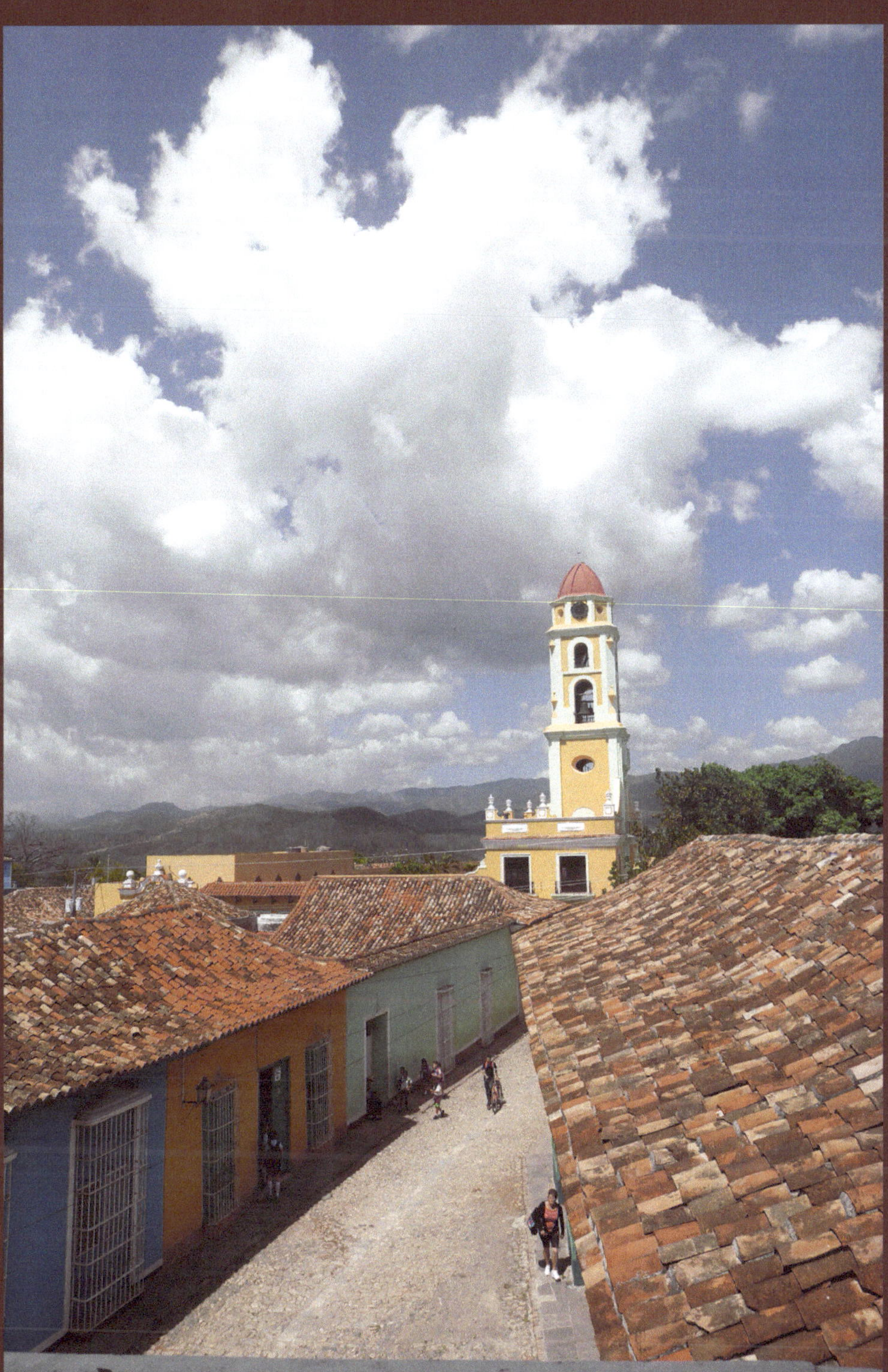

A country scene with a church in the distance

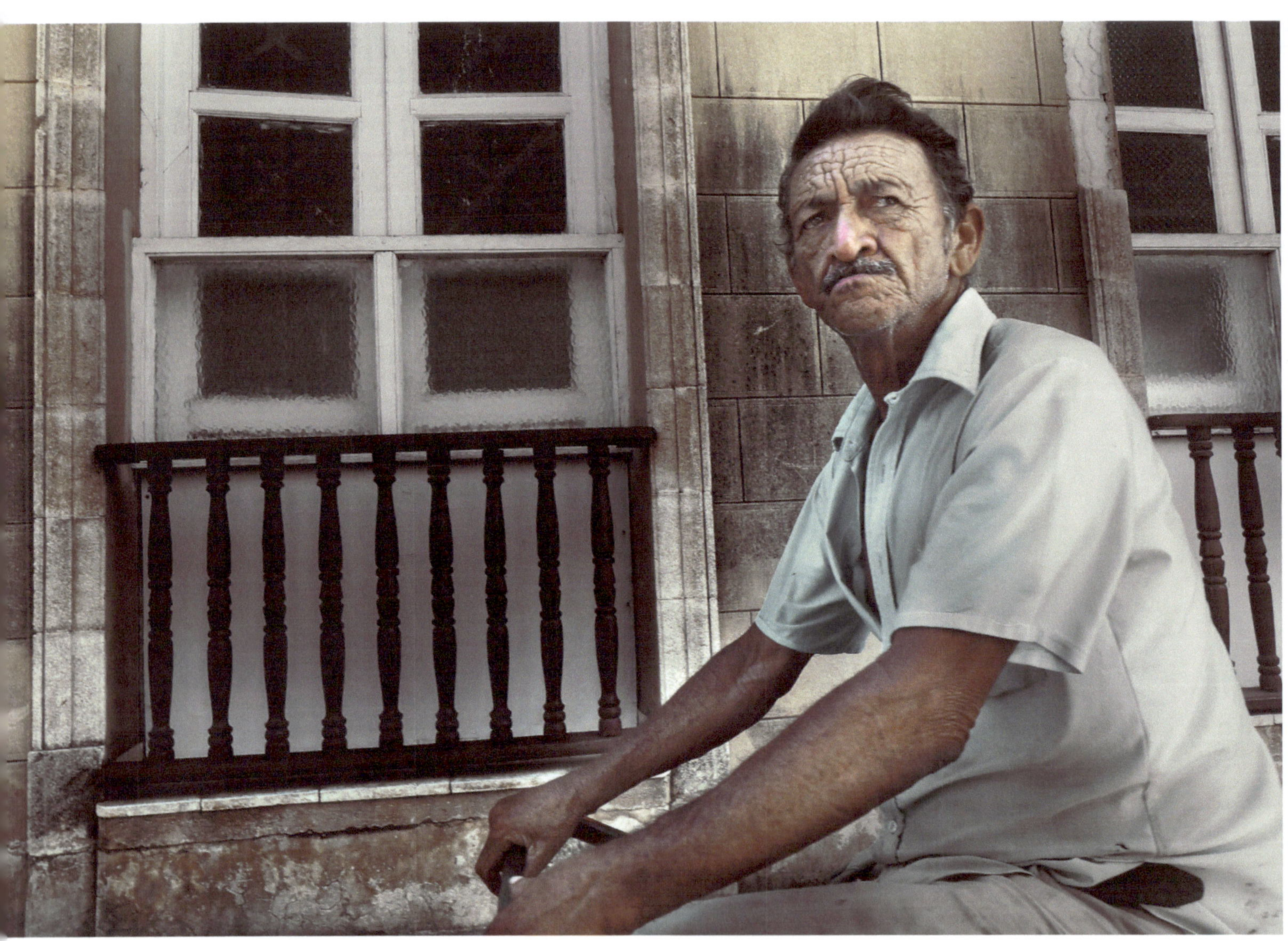

“Men are like the stars; some generate their own light while others reflect the brilliance they receive,” José Martí

School children, the future of Cuba, on their way to class.

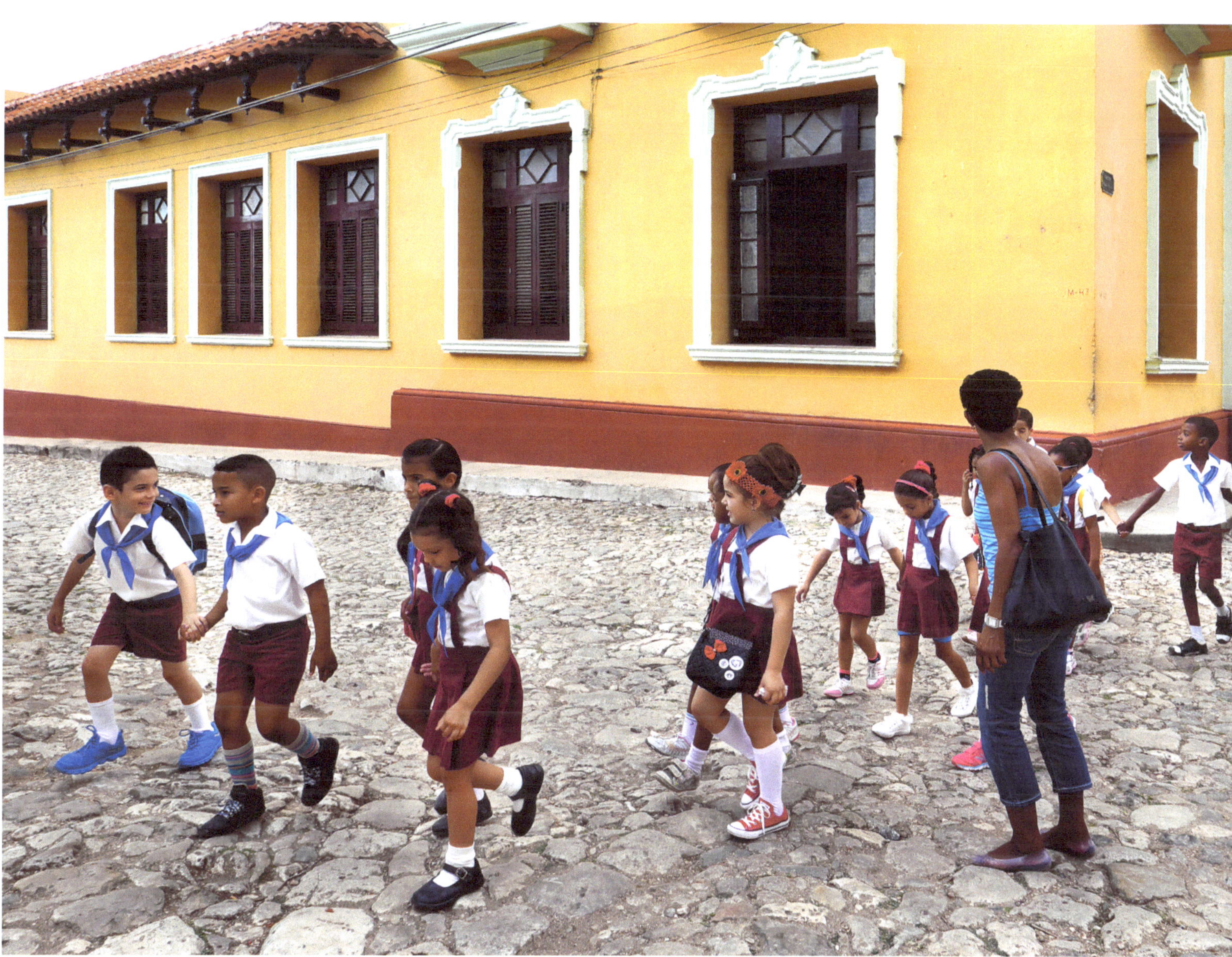

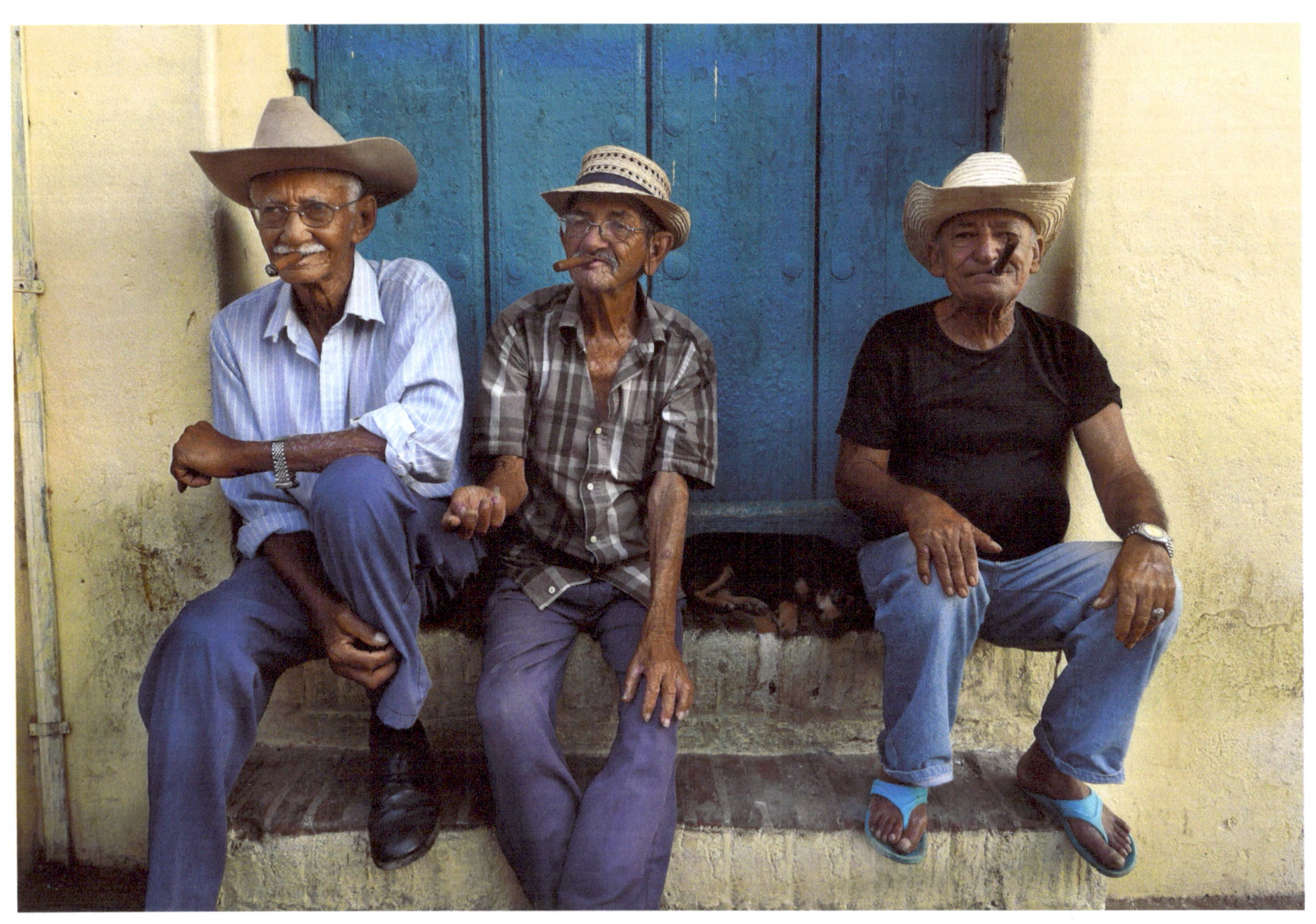

Three men debating the implications of the renewed diplomatic relations between the U.S. and Cuba

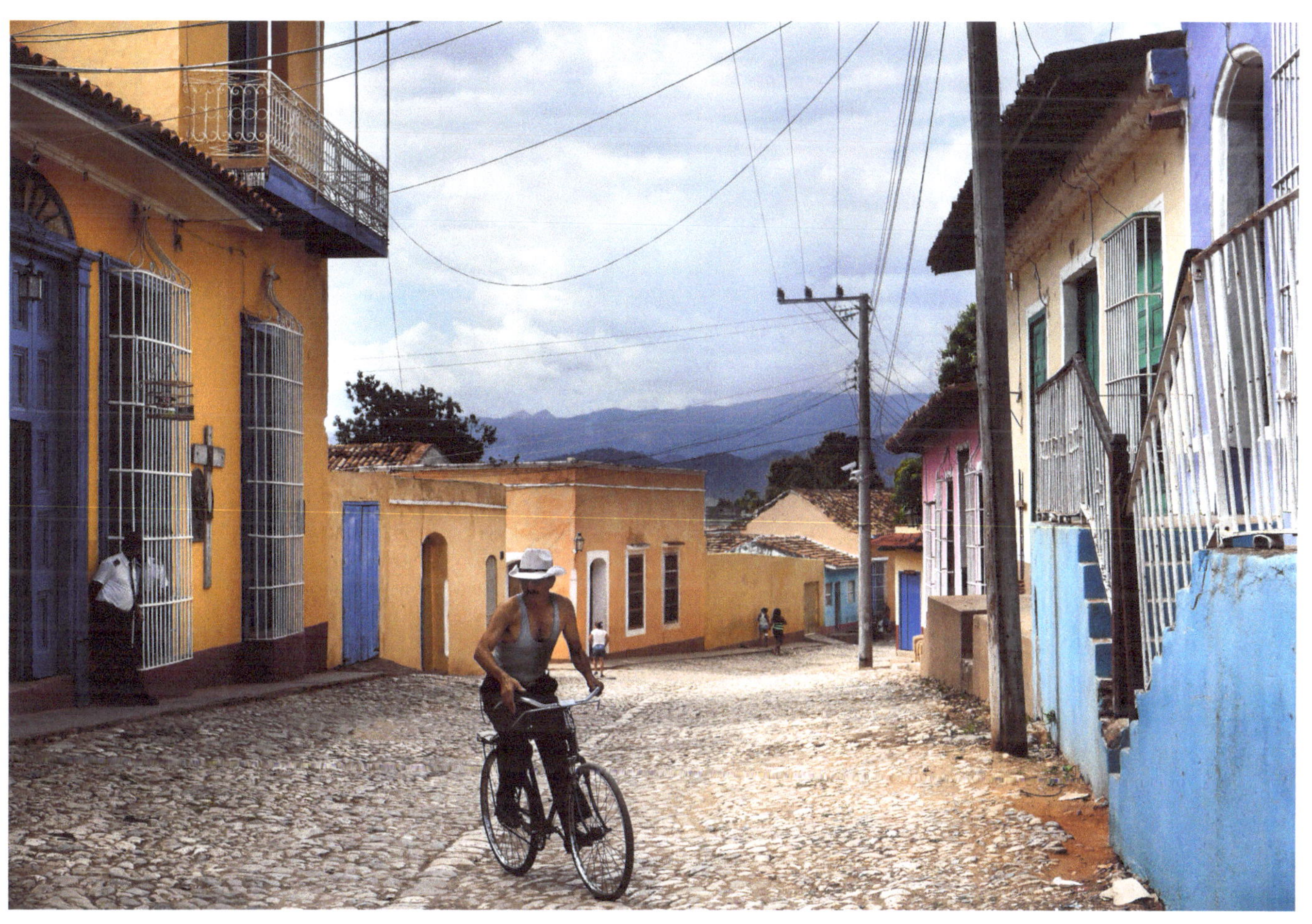

"Me encantaría quererte un poco menos," Maná

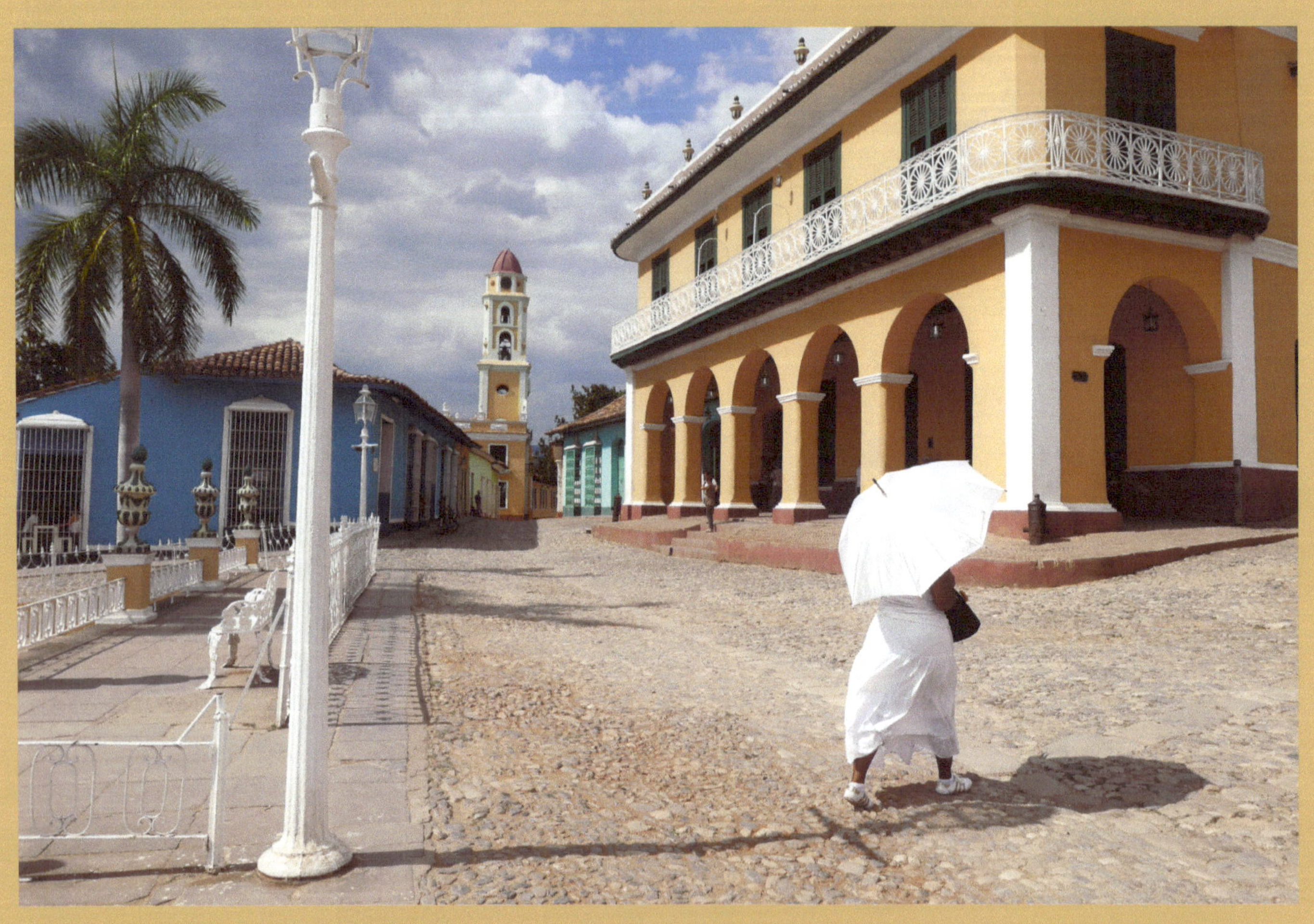

A woman strolls across an empty street in the midday sun

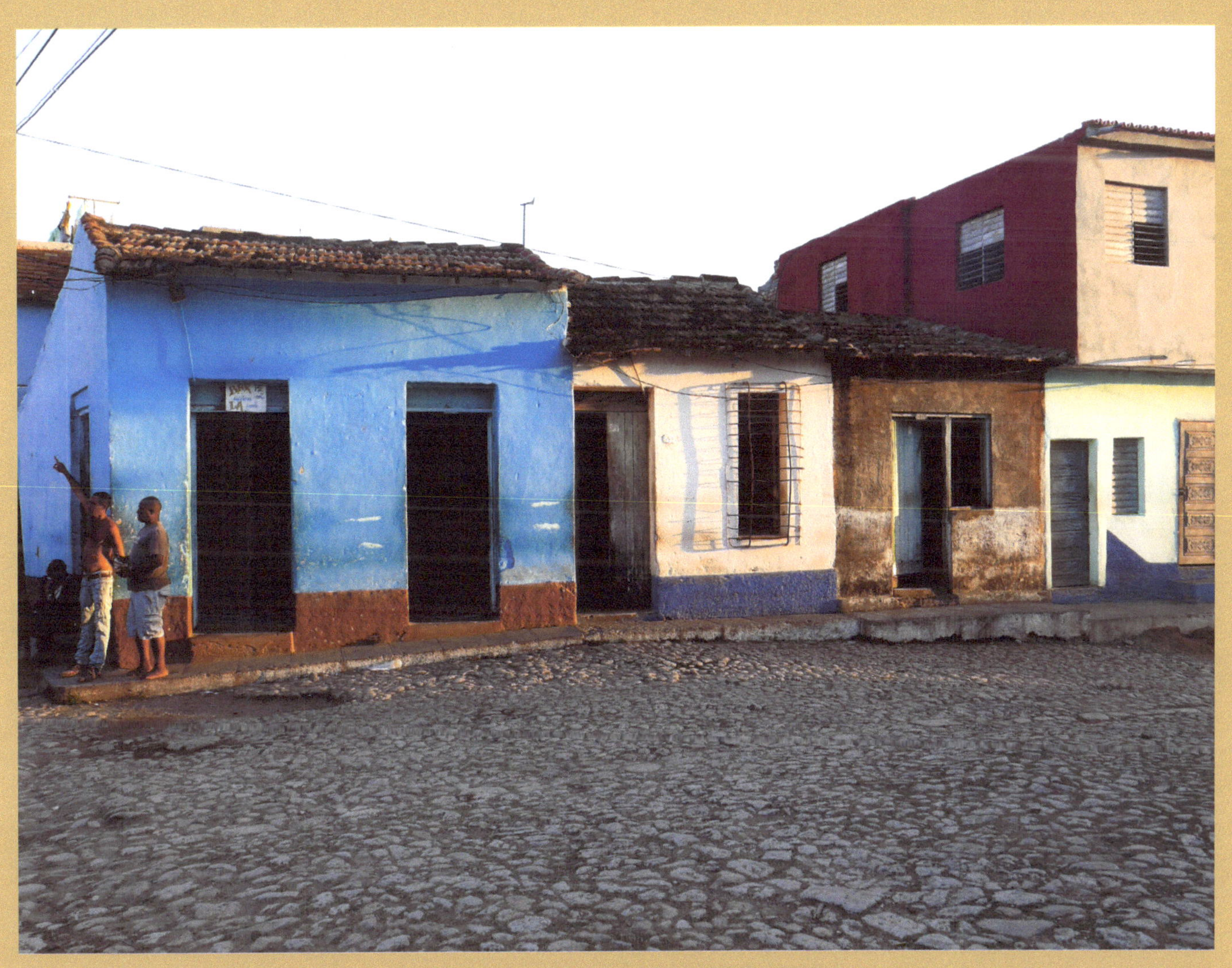

Three men on a corner as dusk arrives

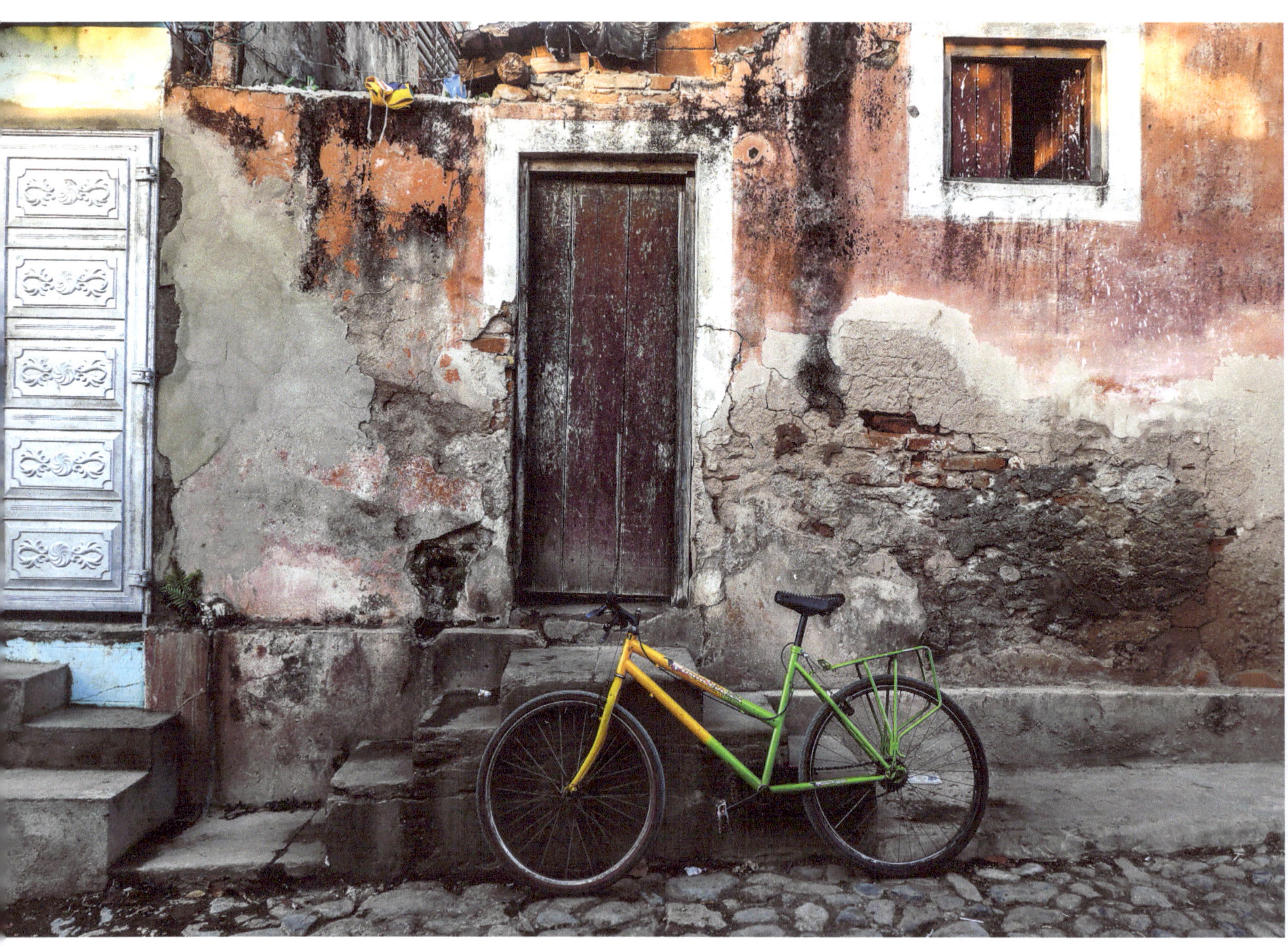

"Life is like riding a bicycle. To keep your balance, you must keep moving," Albert Einstein

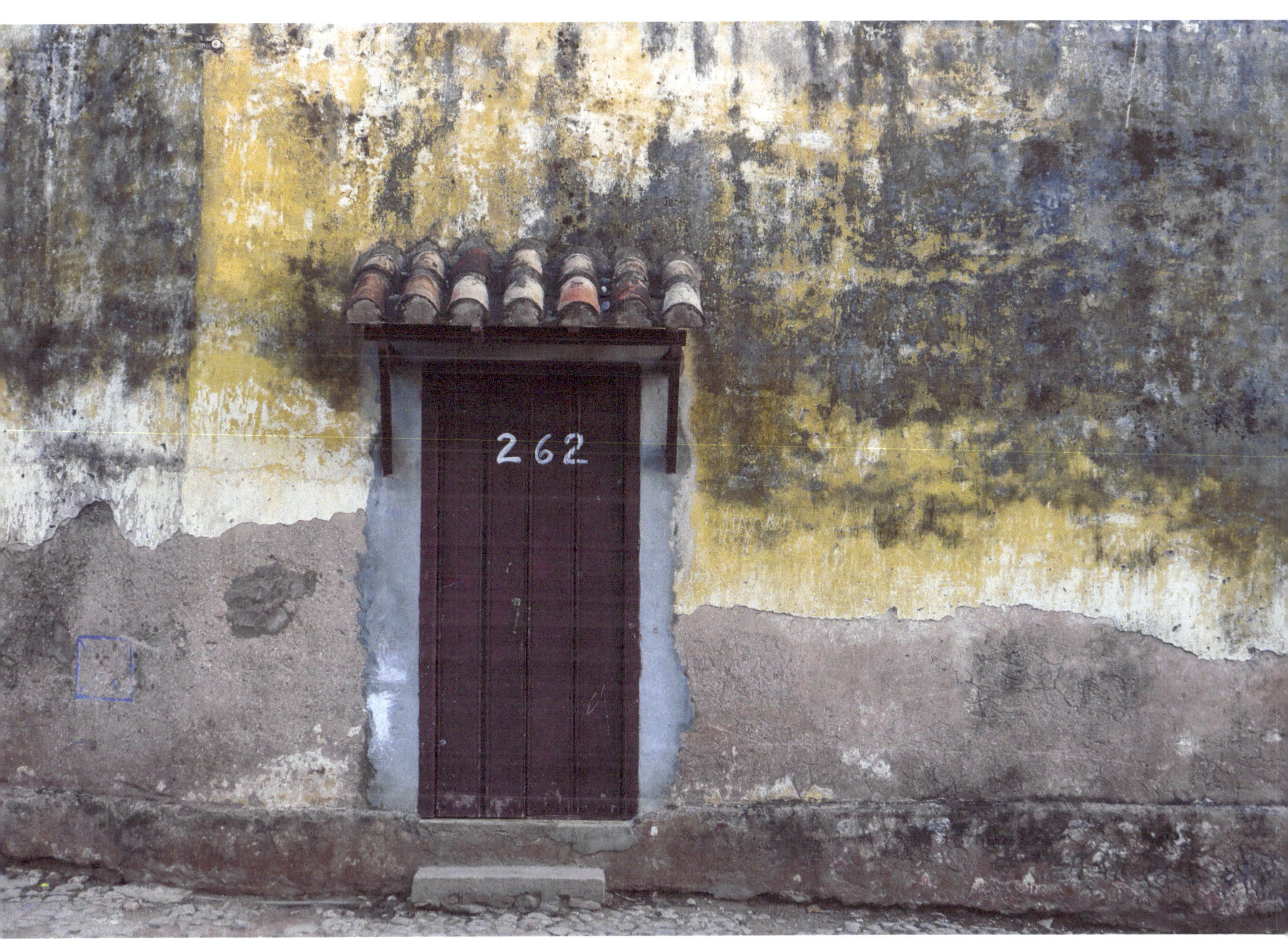

"Until the U.S. agrees to return Guantánamo to us, the door will remain closed," Fidel Castro

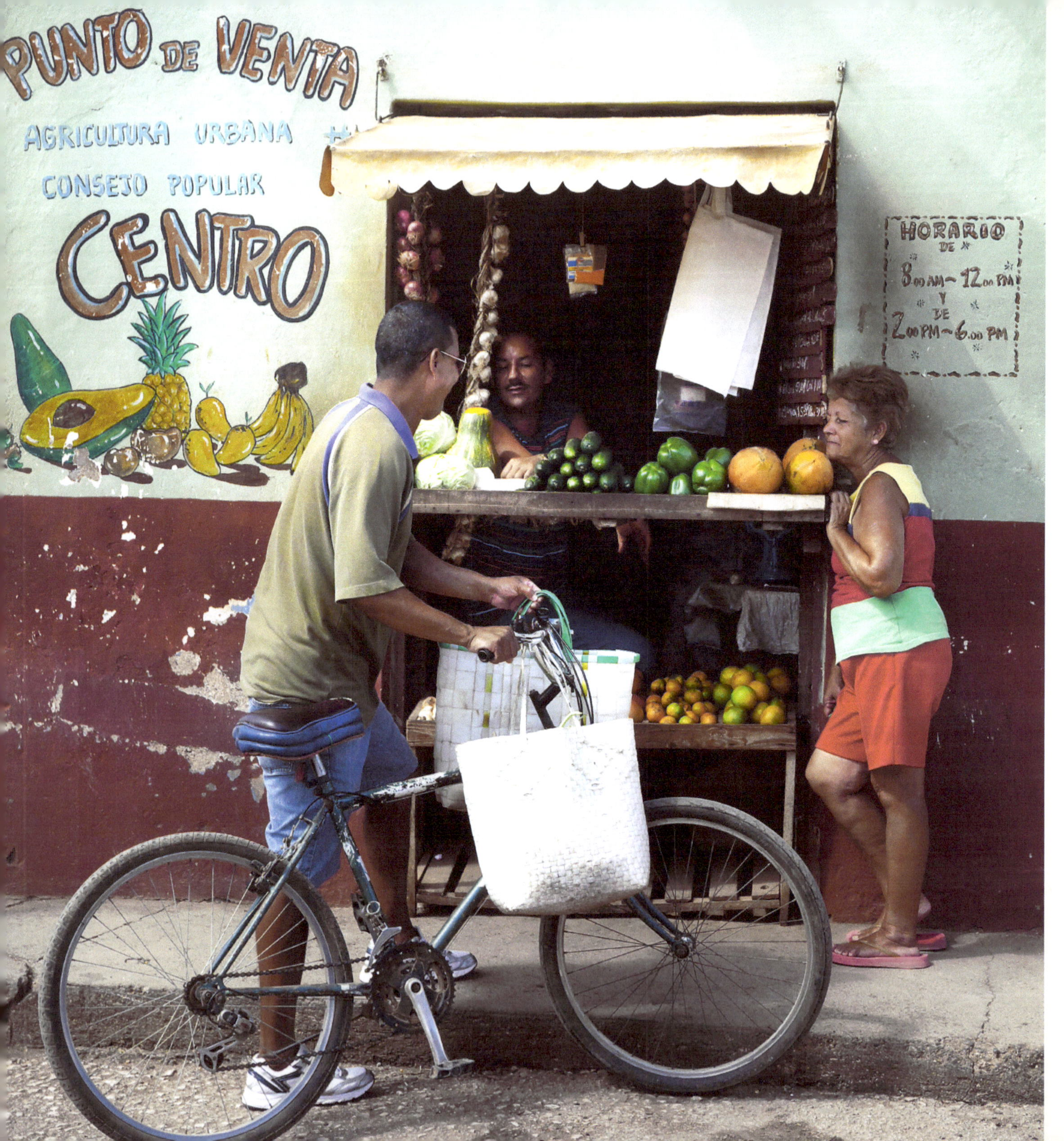
PUNTO DE VENTA
AGRICULTURA URBANA
CONSEJO POPULAR
CENTRO
HORARIO DE
8.00 AM ~ 12.00 PM
Y DE
2.00 PM ~ 6.00 PM

◀

A produce stand in a rural town

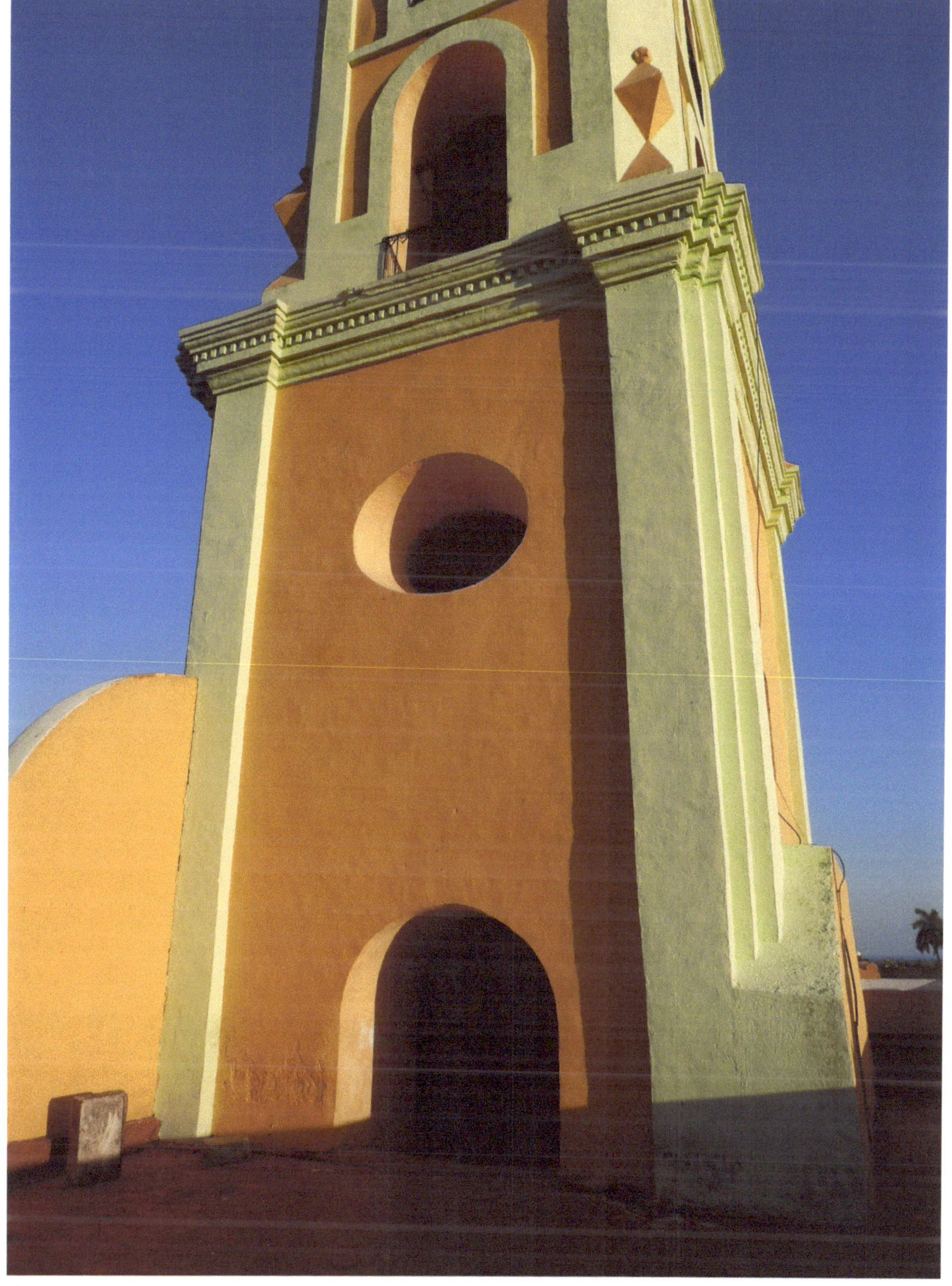

"May Cuba, with all its magnificent potential, open itself up to the world, and may the world open itself up to Cuba," Pope John Paul II

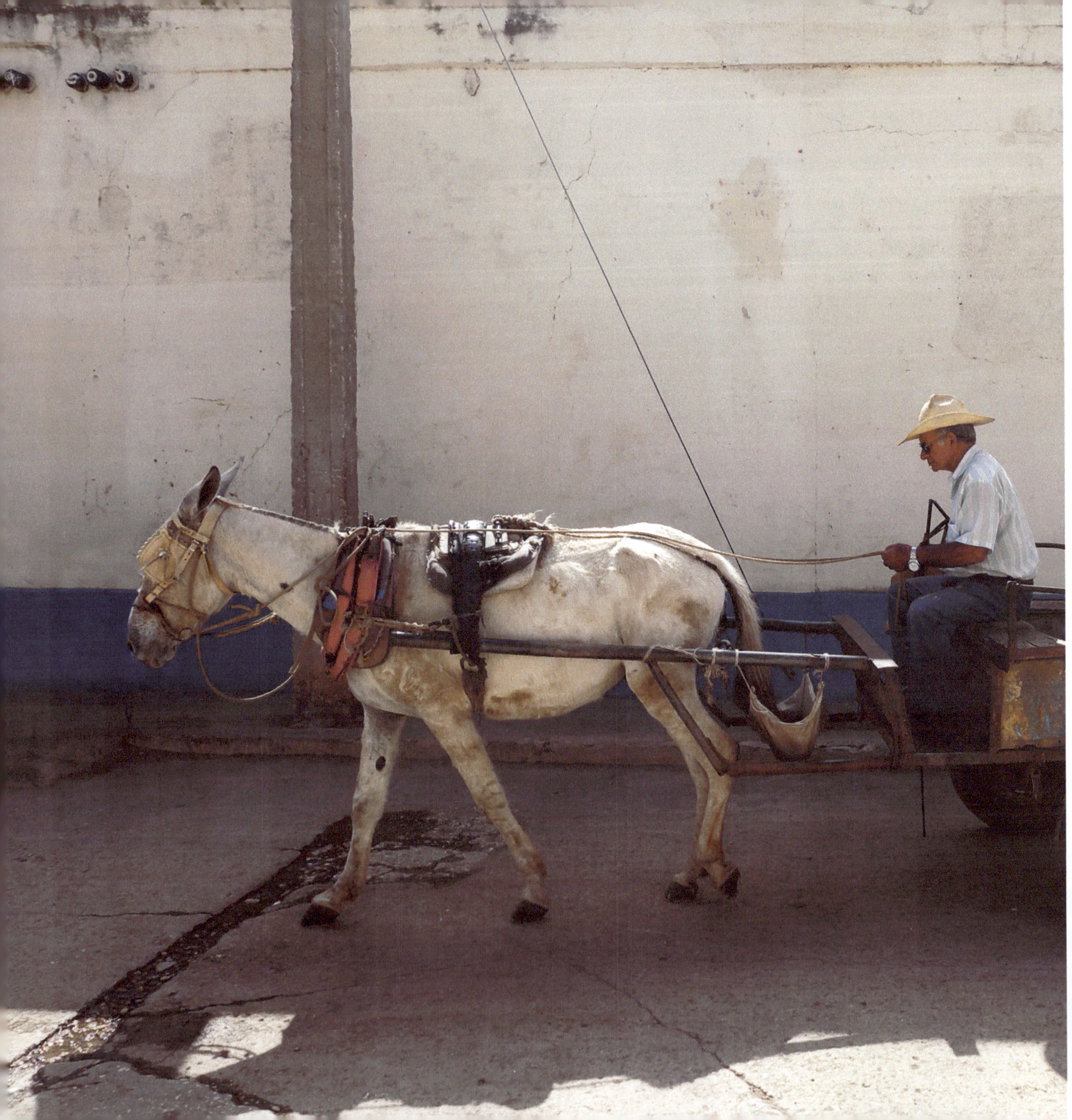

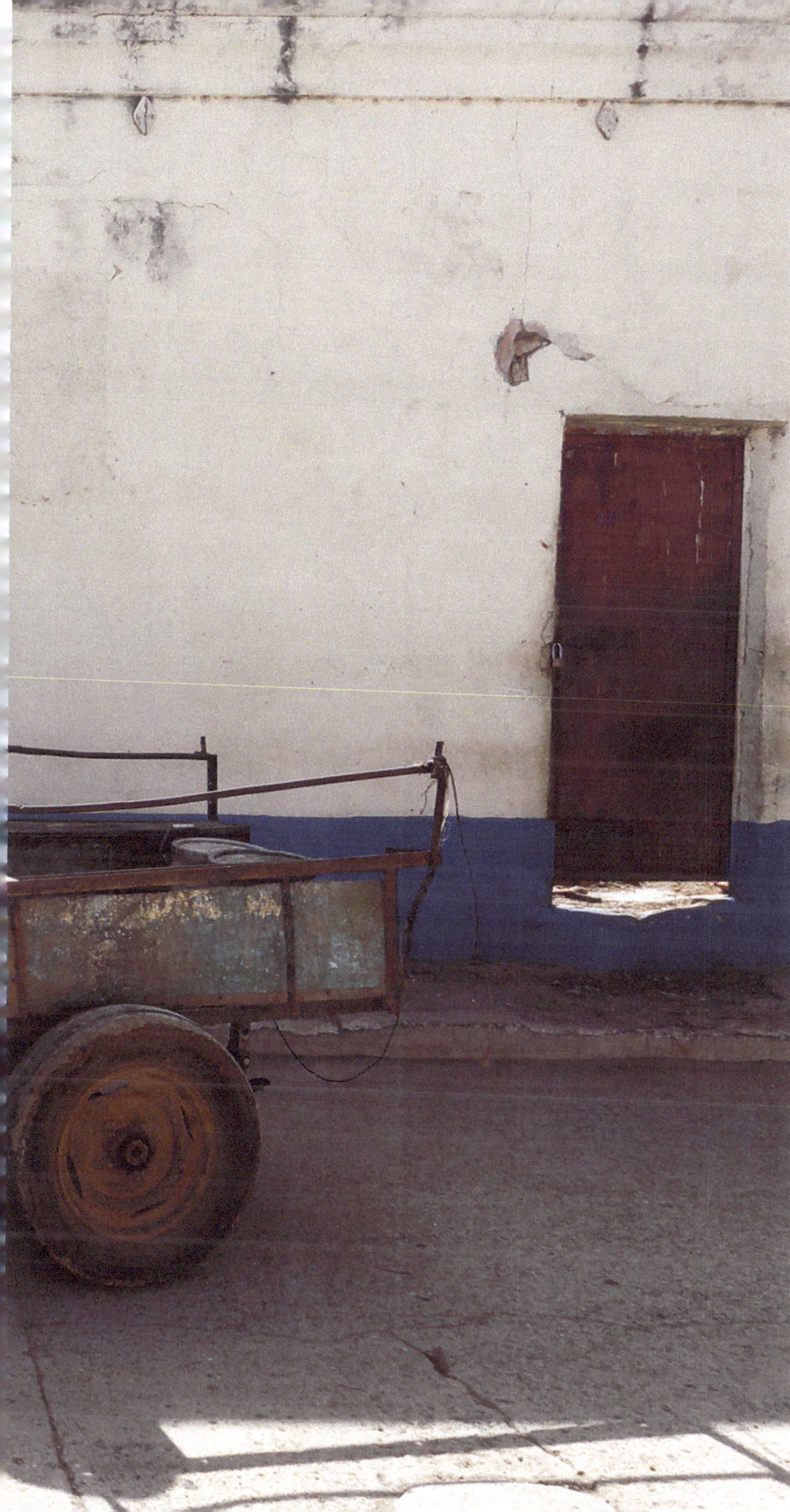

"A revolution is not a bed of roses," Fidel Castro

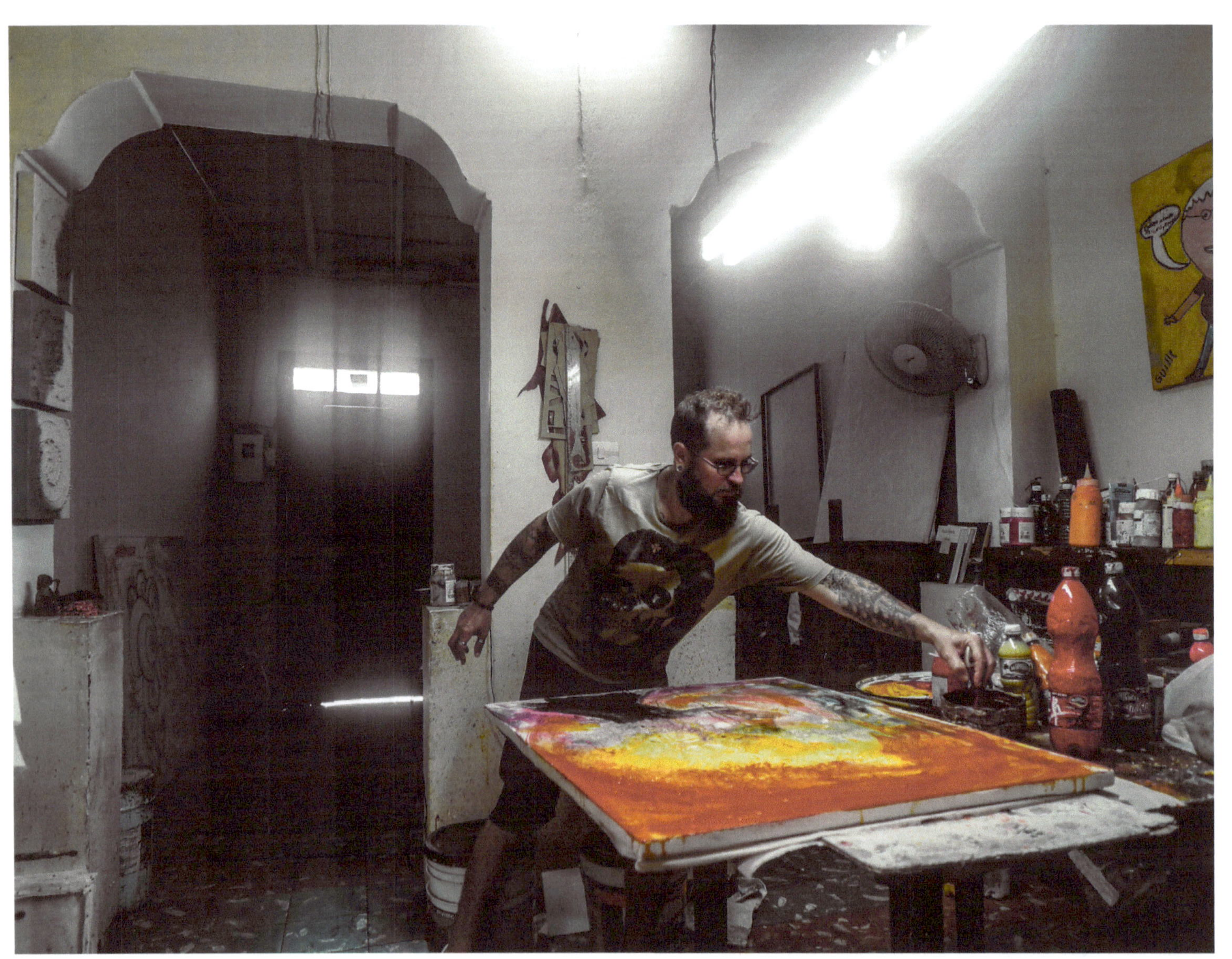

Many Cuban artists, like Idris Rodríguez, are at the forefront of a cultural Renaissance

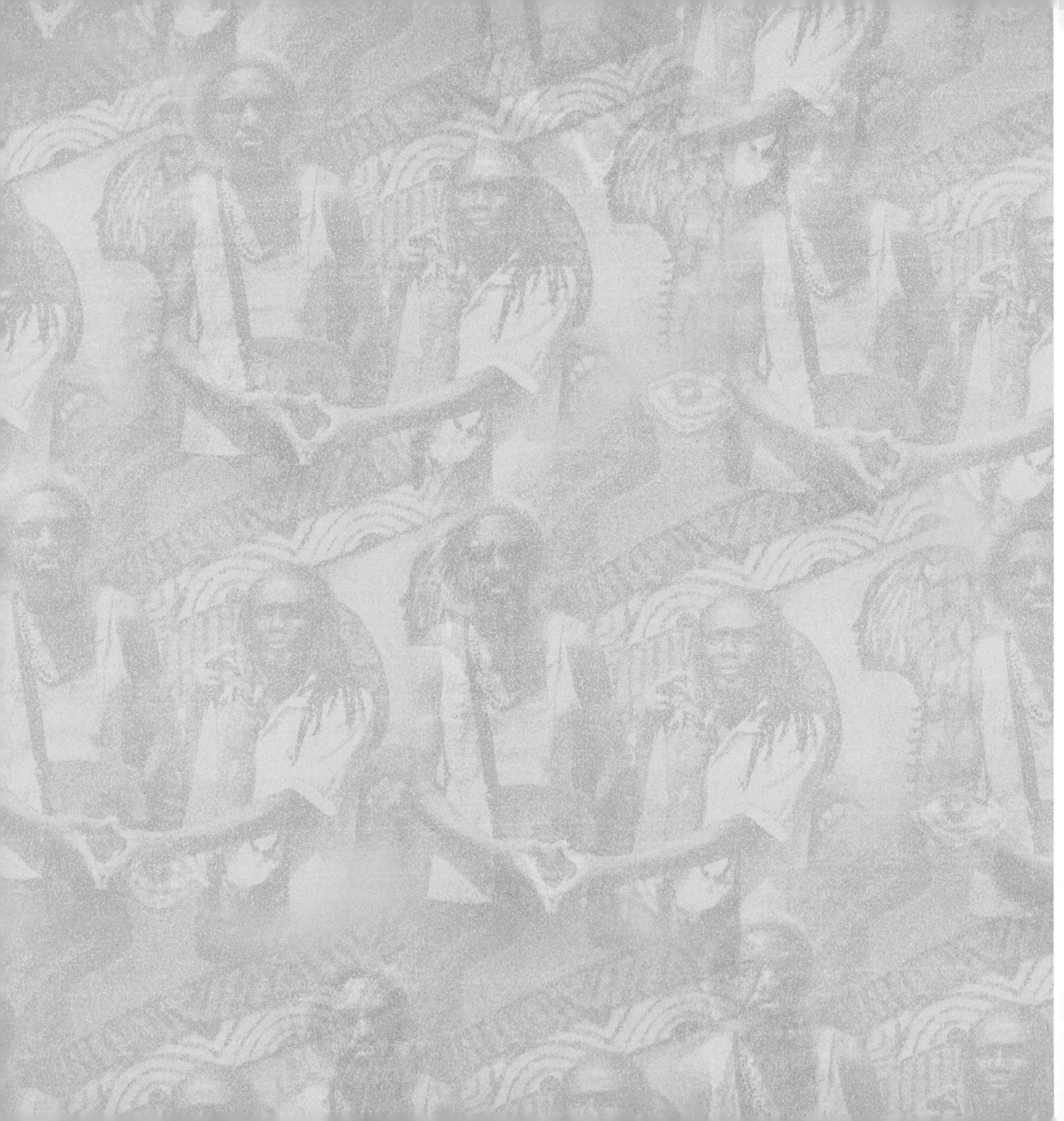

www.ingramcontent.com/pod-product-compliance
Lightning Source LLC
LaVergne TN
LVHW070136110826
845147LV00002B/262

9781939879233